Ending the War on Drugs

Ending the War on Drugs

With an Introduction by
Richard Branson

1 3 5 7 9 10 8 6 4 2

Virgin Books, an imprint of Ebury Publishing,
20 Vauxhall Bridge Road,
London SW1V 2SA

Virgin Books is part of the Penguin Random House group of companies whose addresses
can be found at global.penguinrandomhouse.com

Contributing authors: Pavel Bém, Sam Branson, Fernando Henrique Cardoso, Nick Clegg, Ruth
Dreifuss, Peter Dunne, César, Gaviria, Anand Grover, Professor Carl L. Hart, Michel Kazatchkine,
Olusegun Obasanjo, George Soros, Ernesto Zedillo

First published by Virgin Books in 2016

www.eburypublishing.co.uk

A CIP catalogue record for this book is available from the British Library

ISBN 9780753557464

Typeset in India by Thomson Digital Pvt Ltd, Noida, Delhi

Printed and bound in Great Britain by Clays Ltd, St Ives PLC

Contents

Sir Richard Branson

Sir Richard Branson is the founder of the Virgin Group, one of the world's best-known brands, with operations in diverse sectors from travel to telecommunications, health to banking and music to leisure. Through more than 100 companies worldwide, Virgin employs approximately 60,000 people in over 50 countries.

Since starting youth culture magazine *Student* at the age of 16, Branson has found entrepreneurial ways to provoke positive change in the world. In 2004 he established Virgin Unite, the non-profit foundation of the Virgin Group, which tackles tough social and environmental problems and strives to make business a force for good. An outspoken advocate for reform of global drug laws, he joined the Global Commission on Drug Policy in 2011.

Introduction

· · · · · · · · · · ·

By Sir Richard Branson

Since 2011 I've been a member of the Global Commission on Drug Policy, a group of global leaders from politics, business and civil society advocating a shift in global and national drug policies. It is my work with the Commission that has inspired this book and made me believe that change really can happen.

So I invited some of my fellow Commissioners and a few others, many of whom have spent years on the front lines of the drug war, to share their insights as well as their recommendations. The resulting collection of essays shines a spotlight on the many complex layers of this truly global debate. But no matter what the angle, from the race dimension of the U.S. War on Drugs to New Zealand's approach to so-called 'legal highs', the case for change is overwhelming.

> Despite all the resources spent by governments, the global drugs trade is now entirely controlled by violent criminal organisations

Global spending on drug law enforcement currently exceeds $100 billion per annum – roughly the equivalent of the total amount spent on foreign aid worldwide. However, these huge investments have done nothing to reduce drug production, supply and use. Instead, they have served as seed funding for a vast criminal industry with an estimated annual turnover of $320 billion, eager to meet a growing worldwide demand for illicit drugs. Despite all the resources spent by governments, the global drugs trade is now entirely controlled by violent criminal organisations – including terrorists – that have little concern for the consequences of their actions.

Along the entire supply chain, the War on Drugs has left a trail of destruction and death, violence and insecurity. In Mexico, conservative estimates put the number of people killed in drug-related violence in recent years at more than 100,000; swathes of South and Central America are experiencing unprecedented levels of crime; Afghanistan is a ruined state producing 90 per cent of the world's heroin; and parts of West Africa are so mired in corruption and trafficking that they have virtually no state functions remaining.

How did things go so badly wrong? The 1961 Single Convention on Narcotic Drugs first laid down the concept that drugs – and therefore the people who used, produced or sold them – constituted a threat to humankind. This approach was re-emphasised in 1971 by US President Richard Nixon, when he famously declared a War on Drugs. His idea to 'stem the tide of drug abuse' in the US and beyond by vigorously fighting supply and criminalising demand caught on and spread like wildfire, and by the end of the 1970s most of the world's governments had adopted the same stance. A further convention against trafficking in 1988 consolidated the international framework based on strict law enforcement, zero tolerance and the vision of a drug-free world.

More than four decades on, it has become increasingly clear that this war has been a catastrophic failure. Worse still, the War on Drugs turned out to be a war on people, with dramatic and devastating economic, human and social costs from Bogotá to Brixton, and from Kabul to Kingston. In many countries the death penalty continues to take its toll, and drugs have played a huge role in the rise of mass incarceration. In the US alone, over 1.5 million people were arrested in 2014 on non-violent drug charges, 83 per cent of them solely for possession. Globally, more than one in five people

The War on Drugs turned out to be a war on people, with dramatic and devastating economic, human and social costs

sent to prison are there for drug offences, with minorities and the poor being hit the hardest.

Prohibition has also increased the health risks associated with all drug use. Making drugs illegal pushes the market towards riskier, more potent (and therefore more profitable) products, leads to the use of contaminated drugs of unknown strength, encourages high-risk-using behaviours, pushes consumption into unsafe environments and forces people who use drugs to come into contact with a potentially violent criminal underworld.

It's high time we stop pretending we have any control over drugs. The only way to wrest back control is to end the drug war, take the markets back from criminal networks and put governments in charge, so that drug production, supply and use can be regulated via doctors, pharmacists and licensed retailers. The more dangerous a drug is, the more important that it is properly controlled by the government. Only then can there be a role for legitimate businesses, working as they do now within the legal medicine industry, following safe, accountable systems under the rule of law.

There is proof already that such ways of working are viable and some leaders have already shown the vision and the courage needed to forge ahead. In 2013 Uruguay took matters into its own hands and decided to create a regulated cannabis market. In the US four states have done the same, with more planning to follow suit. In October 2015 Canada's new Prime Minister Justin Trudeau promised to legalise and regulate cannabis, while Ireland's drug policy minister Aodhán Ó Ríordáin recently announced government plans to decriminalise possession for personal use of all drugs.

Other countries have chosen a health-based approach that focuses mainly on the use and possession of drugs. The Netherlands decriminalised the possession of cannabis in 1976 and Portugal decriminalised all drug use in 2001, investing instead in public health services for people who use drugs. This has resulted in some very positive outcomes, such as massive reductions in drug-related deaths and tumbling rates of HIV and hepatitis infections.

These are encouraging and promising developments, but they are almost entirely limited to the West. Too many countries still shy away from any kind of reform, fearful of challenging the status quo and violating international laws they signed up to many years ago.

> A sea change is coming, led by those in Latin America who have paid such a high price over the last five decades and the civil society groups around the world fighting for peace and security

But a sea change is coming, led by those in Latin America who have paid such a high price over the last five decades and the civil society groups around the world fighting for peace and security. Notably, one by one, nine UN agencies have so far called for an end to the war on drug users. In a remarkable about-face, the last one to do so was the UN Office on Drugs and Crime (UNODC), which has shaped and defended global drug policy for decades. In October 2015 it drafted a position paper calling on governments around the world to decriminalise drug use and possession for personal consumption of all drugs. Sadly, the document was withdrawn just prior to release, reportedly due to political pressures. But it added further credence to what many have long said: the War on Drugs has failed. Now is the time to engage with the evidence, review current policy and discuss reforms that could save lives and rescue entire communities.

As the UN General Assembly gears up for the first global drug policy debate in 18 years in April 2016, in preparation for developing a new 10-year international drugs strategy, I hope *Ending the War on Drugs* will inform, enlighten and mobilise those who have been sitting on the fence of this debate thus far. We need champions, advocates and legislators to step forward and demand policies rooted in evidence and common sense.

I encourage you to go to page 183 and take part in the campaigns, contact your political representatives, demonstrate and speak out, because this might be the most important thing you ever do to make the world a better, safer place.

Necker Island, March 2016
Sir Richard Branson

The War on Drugs in numbers

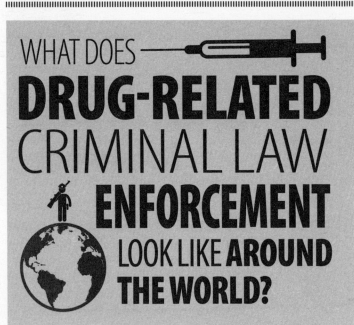

WHAT DOES DRUG-RELATED CRIMINAL LAW ENFORCEMENT LOOK LIKE AROUND THE WORLD?

PUNISHMENT

1.5 MILLION PEOPLE IN THE US WERE ARRESTED IN 2014 ON NON-VIOLENT DRUG CHARGES.

➤ 693,482 people were arrested for a cannabis law violation in 2013.

➤ 88% of these people were subsequently charged with cannabis law violations.

THE US HAS **THE HIGHEST INCARCERATION RATE IN THE WORLD.** 1 IN EVERY 110 AMERICAN ADULTS WAS **INCARCERATED IN 2013** IN FEDERAL, STATE AND LOCAL PRISONS AND JAILS.

ALL ASIAN COUNTRIES IMPRISON PEOPLE FOR DRUG USE, BUT THE DEGREES OF SEVERITY AND STANDARDS DIFFER:

➤ **5** COUNTRIES Impose corporal punishment for drug-related offences, including whipping, caning and flogging.

➤ **10** COUNTRIES require compulsory surveillance and monitoring of individuals arrested for drug use, which can include random and compulsory medical testing for an indefinite period of time.

➤ **12** COUNTRIES detain people for up to three years for drug use, for the purpose of rehabilitation. However, these detention centres have no basis in scientific or medical evidence, and can simply enhance the stigma and discrimination towards people who use drugs.

➤ **16** COUNTRIES impose compulsory registration requirements for people who use drugs. In some cases, this can be used against individuals for the purposes of investigation and interrogation.

➤ **17** COUNTRIES enforce compulsory urine testing for suspected drug use, and a further 6 countries impose involuntary drug testing through medical examinations.

➤ At least **10** COUNTRIES impose mandatory death sentences for drug-related offences.

WHILE SOME COUNTRIES HAVE RECENTLY ABOLISHED **CAPITAL PUNISHMENT** FOR DRUG OFFENCES, IT **INCREASED** FROM 10 COUNTRIES IN 1979 TO 33 COUNTRIES BY 2015.

MORE THAN **350,000 PEOPLE WHO USE DRUGS ARE ESTIMATED TO BE HELD IN DRUG DETENTION CENTRES** IN CAMBODIA, CHINA, LAO PDR AND VIETNAM.

RACIAL DISRIMINATION

5 TIMES AS MANY WHITE AMERICANS ARE USING DRUGS AS AFRICAN AMERICANS.

➡ Yet African Americans are sent to prison for drug offences at **10 times the rate of white Americans.**

African Americans represent 12% of the total population of drug users, but they represent **38% of all people arrested for drug offences**, and 59% of people in state prisons for drug offences.

African Americans serve virtually **as much time in prison for a drug offence** (58.7 months) **as white Americans do for a violent offence** (61.7 months).

HOW HAS DRUG POLICY TO-DATE AFFECTED THE WORLD AROUND US?

INFECTION AND DEATH

MANY COUNTRIES STILL **DO NOT HAVE A NEEDLE AND SYRINGE PROGRAMME** OR OPIOID SUBSTITUTION THERAPY – PROVEN MEASURES FOR REDUCING THE SPREAD OF BLOOD-BORNE INFECTIONS, **INCLUDING HIV AND HEPATITIS C,** AMONG PEOPLE WHO INJECT DRUGS.

75% OF PEOPLE WHO INJECT DRUGS LIVE IN **MIDDLE-INCOME COUNTRIES,** AND 40% OF NEW HIV INFECTIONS IN THESE COUNTRIES ARE RELATED TO **UNSAFE INJECTING.**

AMONG PEOPLE WHO INJECT DRUGS IN PORTUGAL NEW CASES OF HIV INFECTION **FELL DRAMATICALLY** AFTER THEY IMPLEMENTED DECRIMINALISATION AND HARM REDUCTION POLICIES, FROM 1,482 IN 2000 TO 78 IN 2013.

DECRIMINALISATION AND HARM REDUCTION MEASURES HAVE **DRAMATICALLY LOWERED DRUG-RELATED DEATHS** IN COUNTRIES SUCH AS THE CZECH REPUBLIC,

COMPARED TO **HIGH DRUG-RELATED DEATH RATES IN COUNTRIES THAT ENFORCE CRIMINALISATION,** SUCH AS SWEDEN.

90 PER CENT OF COCAINE ENTERING THE US

TRANSITS THROUGH MEXICO.

COLLATERAL DAMAGE

While estimates vary, some put the number of **drug-related homicide deaths in Mexico** between 2007 and 2014 at far **more than 100,000** – a number **even greater, by comparison,** than civilian deaths in Iraq and **Afghanistan** in the same period (103,051).

WHAT IS THE SO-CALLED
WAR ON DRUGS
COSTING US TODAY?

THE US SPENDS MORE THAN **$51 BILLION** ON THE WAR ON DRUGS ANNUALLY.

$2.3 BILLION ANNUALLY IS ESTIMATED BY **UNAIDS** TO BE REQUIRED TO FUND **HIV PREVENTION** AMONG PEOPLE WHO INJECT DRUGS.

Only 7% of this figure was invested by international HIV donors at the last count.

JUST **10%** OF WHAT THE EU CURRENTLY SPENDS ON INCARCERATING PEOPLE FOR DRUG OFFENCES WOULD DOUBLE THE GLOBAL FUND TO FIGHT AIDS, TUBERCULOSIS AND MALARIA'S BIGGEST HARM-REDUCTION ALLOCATION.

IF CURRENTLY ILLEGAL DRUGS IN THE US WERE TAXED AT RATES COMPARABLE TO THOSE ON ALCOHOL AND TOBACCO, TAX REVENUE FROM DRUG LEGALISATION COULD YIELD **$46.7 BILLION** ANNUALLY.

Sources can be found on p.192–3.

Ernesto Zedillo

Ernesto Zedillo is the Director of the Yale Center for the Study of Globalization; Professor in the Field of International Economics and Politics; Professor of International and Area Studies; and Professor Adjunct of Forestry and Environmental Studies at Yale University.

He earned his Bachelor's degree from the School of Economics of the National Polytechnic Institute in Mexico and his MA and PhD at Yale University. From 1987 to 1988 he served the National Government of Mexico as Undersecretary of Budget; from 1988 to 1992 as Secretary of Economic Programming and the Budget; and he was appointed Secretary of Education in 1992. In 1994 Zedillo ran for the presidency and won. He served his country as President of Mexico from 1994 to 2000.

Since 2002 he has served on numerous international commissions and task forces, contributed to their respective reports, edited several published volumes, and taught undergraduate courses in the department of economics at Yale.

Zedillo serves on the Global Commission on Drug Policy and is a member of The Elders.

Drug Policy: A Shameful Failure of Modern Civilisation

• • • • • • • • • • • • • • • • •

By Ernesto Zedillo

The amazing progress that a substantial portion of
humanity has enjoyed in its recent history has been fundamentally
a consequence of the various revolutions in human knowledge that
have ensued since the original scientific revolution of the sixteenth
and seventeenth centuries. The unprecedented advance in standards
of living that occurred over the last two centuries throughout most
of the world has been driven by the generation, dissemination
and application of knowledge. Every day, that knowledge touches
every aspect of human life practically everywhere on the planet. The
accumulation of greater human knowledge has not been limited
strictly to the scientific and technological. Considerable progress has
also been made in the expansion of knowledge dedicated to better
organisation of the production and consumption of the goods and
services made possible by technology and human accomplishments.
And, of course, knowledge accumulated since the Enlightenment and
the scientific revolution has also decisively shaped the culture, values
and governances of modern societies.

Unfortunately, the impact of knowledge on governance, and the
resulting policies, have been uneven, frequently muted or, even worse,
cast aside outright by policies that openly fall foul of that very same
knowledge. In many areas with significant human consequences, there
is a stark disconnect between the public policies applied and what
knowledge would advise based on both scientific inquiry and practical
experience. This is sheer folly, and examples abound; but a particularly
conspicuous one is provided by the case of drug policy throughout
the world.

In a nutshell, for too long and with far too few exceptions, drug
policies have relied fundamentally on prohibition and law enforcement.
This approach is wholly inconsistent with the best knowledge from life
sciences, sound public health research and economic analysis.

Paradoxically, some of the best knowledge on drug abuse and addiction has been generated by the very same government institutions that have also failed to apply that knowledge to their drug policies. For example, the National Institute on Drug Abuse (NIDA) is an excellent research institution of the US federal government, which has done much to advance the understanding of drug use. On its website, NIDA informs us with remarkable clarity and simplicity what science knows about why people begin taking drugs and why some people become addicted to drugs. This essential scientific knowledge should make it clearly understood that even if the best possible prevention strategies were applied – which unfortunately has never been the case – there would still be a residual demand for drugs irrespective of whether they are prohibited or even highly priced in whatever market they are available.

> Some of the best knowledge on drug abuse and addiction has been generated by the very same government institutions that have also failed to apply that knowledge to their drug policies

For its part, economic analysis demonstrates that prohibiting the production and consumption of any merchandise for which demand exists invariably leads to the creation of a black market by individuals and organisations willing to violate the law. Significantly, economic analysis also indicates that decriminalising the use and production of a prohibited drug and taxing its consumption would cause a greater reduction in its output than the enforcement of its prohibition (even if enforcement were aimed at an optimal, although in practice most likely unachievable, level).

And yet for over a century, prohibition – and its intended enforcement – have prevailed as the preferred policy approach for dealing with the consumption of drugs. This approach, initially adopted for only a few drugs by a certain number of countries, was progressively extended to cover many more substances and eventually universalised through successive international conventions that have been complemented by bi-national or regional agreements. What is remarkable about the origin, spread and prevalence of the prohibition and enforcement approach is how inconsistent it has proved to be, not only with the best knowledge but also with the results that such a policy has actually delivered in practice.

Looking at the history of drug policy it is tempting to conclude that most of the time it has been driven essentially by ill-informed politics. This is certainly the case for the country that has been most influential in the construction of the existing international regime for drug policy, the United States. The history of US drug policy seems to have been shaped over time much more by the ideological propensities of individuals in positions of power – and their purely tactical political objectives, partisan politics, bureaucratic disputes among government departments, short-sighted foreign policy objectives, sometimes even ethnic and racial misperceptions – and much less, if ever, by the objective of reducing the harm caused by the production, sale and consumption of drugs in the population.

> The history of US drug policy seems to have been shaped over time ... by the ideological propensities of individuals in positions of power

That history was well documented by the late Professor David Musto of Yale University, who in several of his scholarly writings reminds us that the outlawing of opium in 1909 and passage of the Harrison Act in 1914 were partly an irrational and racist reaction towards some population groups. The opium ban reflected that drug's association with Chinese immigrant railroad workers in the West, and the Harrison Act responded to some Southerners' alleged fear that 'cocaine crazed African Americans might attack white society', a racist attitude that interestingly coincided with the peak of lynching, legal segregation and discriminatory voting laws.

He also documented that a narcotics committee appointed by the US Treasury Department to study the problem of control and to recommend changes to the law concluded, without providing any sound supporting evidence, that 'addicts are weak creatures, lacking in moral sense, and when deprived of their drug [they] may commit crime in order to obtain it'. This rather prejudiced and uninformed opinion was released to the public in 1919 and continued to influence policy from then on, despite the fact that many in the medical profession were already admitting publicly that drug addiction was a physical disease and not the result of 'weak willpower'. Instead of listening to the medical professionals, the US Justice Department indicted doctors who issued prescriptions for maintenance purposes for violation of federal narcotic laws.

The Federal Bureau of Narcotics (FBN) was created in 1930, when the incorrect idea that drug use caused criminal behaviour had become firmly and officially entrenched. Around that time, as a consequence of the Depression, immigrants were increasingly unwelcome in the United States. Mexicans in particular became linked with violence and with growing and smoking cannabis, an argument that was also used to carry out their mass deportation. It did not take long before the Marijuana Tax Act, prohibiting the sale, barter or transfer of cannabis between private citizens, became US law in 1937.

Never mind that the wisdom of this policy was questioned rather soon by not a few sensible voices. In the 1940s New York Mayor Fiorello LaGuardia's Committee on Marijuana (with members from the New York Academy of Medicine) reported that:

the marijuana user does not come from the hardened criminal class and there was found no direct relationship between the commission of crimes of violence and marijuana.

The FBN agents and administrators were livid, strongly minimising the report's findings before the media and the general public. Musto mentions that the FBN was instrumental in getting the *Journal of the American Medical Association* to attack the report in an editorial that concluded, 'Public officials will do well to disregard this unscientific, uncritical study, and continue to regard marijuana as a menace wherever it is purveyed.'

Curiously, a few years later the very same American Medical Association (AMA) allied with the American Bar Association (ABA) to create a joint committee to study narcotics and the drug problem. The committee's report, published in 1961, pointed out that:

> *some responsible authorities state that the physical and psychological dependence of addicts on narcotic drugs, the compulsion to obtain them, and the high price of drugs in the illicit market are predominantly responsible for the crimes committed by addicts and others claim that the drug itself is responsible for criminal behavior,*

and concluded that:

> *the weight of evidence is so heavily in favor of the former point of view that the question can hardly be called a controversial one.*

Here, backed by scientific research, are two authoritative institutions explaining that forcing drug users to rely on the black market – a market actually created by the policies themselves – and not the drugs, were at the root of the criminal problem. To further contradict the rationale of those policies, the AMA–ABA committee argued:

> *In terms of numbers afflicted, and in ill effects on others in the community, drug addiction is a problem of far less magnitude than alcoholism. Crimes of violence are rarely, and sexual crimes are almost never, committed by addicts.*

The FBN, again livid, counter-attacked with its own report placing the members of the AMA–ABA joint committee in the category of 'crackpot' doctors and sociologists.

The FBN's aggressiveness did not discourage the experts. The Presidential Advisory Commission on Narcotic and Drug Abuse, established during the Kennedy administration, recommended in its 1963 report multiple suggestions for the rehabilitation of drug abusers, the relaxation of mandatory minimum sentences, increased appropriation for research and the dismantling of the FBN. Admittedly, that Commission also insisted that the illegal traffic in drugs should be attacked with the full power of the US federal government.

In fact, however, any hope that US drug policy might move away from an essentially repressive approach was soon all but extinguished. Just as drug use suddenly increased among the young during the second half of the 1960s – not least among American military personnel in Vietnam – the prohibitionists got their biggest champion when Richard Nixon was elected President of the United States. Just six months after taking office, on 14 July 1969, President Nixon addressed the US congress on the issue of illegal drugs, and subsequently the War on Drugs began to take shape.

There is plenty of evidence that declaring the War on Drugs was essentially a political decision with total disregard for medical or other pertinent scientific considerations about the problem. Although it took place in June 1971, when some major initiatives on drug policy had already been launched by that administration, a conversation between Nixon and two of his closest advisers, John Ehrlichman and H. R. Haldeman, is highly suggestive of what was motivating the US President to sustain his drug policy pursuit. Haldeman recalled that conversation as follows:

He also told Ehrlichman to sit down and pick out the three main issues that really matter. He commented that revenue sharing only matters if it is tied to tax reduction, and welfare reform only if it related to getting people off of welfare. He emphasized that we shouldn't be concerned if it is something we will actually accomplish and pointed out that JFK was doing all of his progress building on phony issues. Rather, we should look in terms of how we create issues. We need an enemy. We need controversy. We need to do something that will build those things. Drugs and law enforcement may be one, especially since we are so weak in our standing in the polls on those.

It should come as no surprise how Nixon reacted to the report by the National Commission on Marijuana and Drug Abuse created by himself and Congress in 1970. The Commission, actually chaired by a Republican governor, was mandated to re-evaluate cannabis, its characteristics and demographics of use, and what should be done about it. Contrary to Nixon's very public opinion, the Commission's report de-emphasised cannabis as a problem, stated that the social and legal policies were out of proportion to the harm engendered by drug use and recommended decriminalisation of possession of cannabis for personal use on both state and federal levels. In March 1972 Nixon refused to accept the National Commission's final report, stating, 'I oppose the legalization of marijuana and that includes its sale, its possession and its use. I do not believe you can have effective criminal justice based on the philosophy that something is half legal and half illegal. That is my position, despite what the commission has recommended.'

There was some moderation of the Nixon era policies during President Jimmy Carter's administration, but this mild shift was short-lived. Under his successor, President Ronald Reagan, the War on Drugs was back on, including the rejection of any leniency towards consumption.

Although the rhetoric has changed in recent years, along with some significant changes in some states, US federal drug policies have remained essentially within the framework of the Nixon War on Drugs approach.

This policy stability is remarkable considering that its results have been far from satisfactory, despite the immense fiscal cost of its intended and unsuccessful enforcement. Needless to say, the objective of a US free of drugs has proved illusory.

> The attempt to enforce prohibition through the criminal justice system has led to mass incarceration, resulting in nearly half a million people currently serving jail time for drug offences

Not only has the US drug policy failed to diminish in any significant way the market for illegal drugs, but it has also brought about other deeply adverse social consequences. For example, the attempt to enforce prohibition through the criminal justice system has led to mass incarceration, resulting in nearly half a million people currently serving jail time for drug offences. In fact, the US has the highest incarceration rate in the world. Despite recent efforts to reduce the numbers of those imprisoned, there were as many as 2.2 million individuals in jail in 2013, as compared with 300,000 in 1972. Consequently, in the US about 1 out of 100 adults is currently in jail or prison, and 1 out of 31 adults is incarcerated, on probation or on parole.

According to the experts, enforcement of drug policy has proved to be socially discriminatory against the poor. It is particularly detrimental to African Americans, who comprise only 14 per cent of regular drug users, but constitute 37 per cent of those arrested for drug offences and 56 per cent of those imprisoned for drug crimes.

Despite its unsatisfactory results in reducing trafficking and the consumption of drugs and the exceedingly high human and economic costs in the United States, this country's policy has become not only *de facto* but also *de jure* the international approach to dealing with the illicit drug problem. The faulty model has been enshrined in three United Nations Conventions that frame national illicit drug regimes across the globe. Additionally the US has made it a hallmark of its foreign policy to agree to special enforcement mechanisms with countries considered key in the illicit traffic of drugs to its own domestic market.

As expected, since the prohibition and punitive model has failed to achieve its objectives in the US and other highly developed countries, it is not the least surprising that the model has proved to be not only ineffective, but actually disastrous, in countries with weaker institutions and fewer economic resources to enforce the rule of law. Many cases come to mind, unfortunately some of the most extreme in Latin America. Colombia, for one, has endured the loss of more than 200,000 people killed as a consequence of the violence of both organised crime and radical political movements – sometimes acting in symbiosis – and the government's actions to combat them. It took many years and vast resources – both domestic and those provided by the United States through Plan Colombia – to reduce the violence displayed by the criminal groups. Nevertheless, as far as its consequences on the supply of drugs are concerned, the impact of Plan Colombia seems to have been rather modest.

> Colombia, for one, has endured the loss of more than 200,000 people killed as a consequence of the violence of both organised crime and radical political movements

Furthermore, as the security situation started to improve in Colombia, more markedly in the second half of the first decade of this century, Mexico began to suffer an epidemic of organised crime-related violence of proportions unprecedented in the country's history.

Experts have yet to agree on the precise reasons behind this explosion of violent criminality but, without claiming to know the direction of causality, it is clear that such an explosion happened as the Mexican criminal gangs somehow displaced their Colombian counterparts in controlling the most profitable markets while at the same time the Mexican government attempted to tighten its grip on drug traffic and organised crime.

The confluence of these and other factors has been devastating for Mexico. And yet, for one thing, there is zero evidence that the supply of drugs going to the domestic American market was reduced at all, despite the greater law enforcement resources applied by the Mexican government and complemented by those provided by the US through the so-called Plan Merida. Furthermore, far from shrinking, drug trafficking directed to the Mexican market increased. The domestic consumption of illegal drugs has increased since the Mexican War on Drugs was intensified.

90,772 people have died in organised crime-related violence between December 2006 and November 2015

But by far the highest price paid by Mexico is the extraordinary number of deaths brought about by gang-related violence. Eduardo Guerrero, a prestigious Mexican analyst, has carefully calculated that 90,772 people have died in organised crime-related violence between December 2006 and November 2015. Obviously, these are figures only comparable to major warfare. The War on Drugs in Mexico is no longer just a metaphor; it has become exactly that – a war.

Equally worrying is the effect that organised crime has very likely had on the quality of Mexican security and justice institutions. Given organised crime's immense economic power and proven propensity for violence, as well as the fact that those institutions were not particularly strong to begin with, it is not outlandish to assume that they have been further infected by the disease of corruption. Looking forward, this circumstance will make it very hard, if not impossible, for the current approach to drug policy to have any meaningful chance of success in Mexico. Extreme violence may be somewhat reduced, as has happened in very recent years; trafficking routes may be deviated towards Central America and the Caribbean, simultaneously worsening the security problems that these smaller and poorer nations already endure; and domestic drug consumption may be stabilised, but all of this can only happen at an immense sustained economic and human cost. And yet the risk of additional explosions in homicidal violence and further institutional erosion will remain as long as there is not a fundamental revision of the national and international approach to drug policy. Tragically, neither of these changes is yet clearly on the horizon.

> The risk of additional explosions in homicidal violence and further institutional erosion will remain as long as there is not a fundamental revision of the national and international approach to drug policy

True, the debate on drugs policy has been more open and intense over the last few years and some steps towards adopting policies that conform more with what science and experience would recommend have been taken in some places, even in the United States – albeit in only a few jurisdictions. But the pace of reform is too slow – and continually encounters significant obstacles – to allow such progress to be sufficient first to stop and then to reverse the damage that has been endured for too long. While advocates of serious reform have been accommodating of a gradualist approach, forces opposing it have proved to be extremely recalcitrant, despite the evidence in support of such reform.

I have been part of that reformist camp willing to accept that changes in the dominant policies may possibly only happen in incremental steps. When in public office, I pursued the policies dictated both by existing Mexican laws and by the international commitments that had been taken by my country at the multilateral and regional levels – most significantly with the United States. But at the same time our government worked with other governments to try to change the international framework. In this spirit we played a key role in the promotion and preparation of the 1998 United Nations General Assembly Special Session on drugs. Although, along with other like-minded governments such as Portugal, we got the documents emerging from the Special Session to recognise that the existing regime put too much of the responsibility for the problem on those countries involved in supply and not enough on those countries representing the bulk of the demand, any reconsideration of the international conventions that ruled then – and now – remained out of the question. Overall, the Special Session of 1998 proved to be a failed and rather frustrating attempt towards gradual reform. We found that the opponents of any significant change were not only the countries that traditionally championed the prohibitionist approach but, to our dismay, also some bureaucratic entities within the United Nations system that seemingly had developed a strong vested interest in deterring any reformist attempt.

I continued to abide by the gradualist approach to reform as a member of the Latin American Commission on Drugs and Democracy created 10 years after the UNGASS of 1998. Although our final statement was clear in declaring the War on Drugs a failure and advocating that drug use should be treated first and foremost as a matter of public health, we still refrained from suggesting that the international regime be scrapped. Nevertheless, our report contained recommendations that have become focal points in the recent drug policy debate. Rather timidly (although perhaps it seemed bold in February 2009, when the report was issued) we proposed to 'evaluate from a public health standpoint and on the basis of the most advanced medical science the convenience of decriminalizing the possession of cannabis for personal use'. We also said:

The enormous capacity of the narcotics trade for violence and corruption can only be effectively countered if its sources of income are substantially weakened. To accomplish this goal, the State must establish the laws, institutions and regulations enabling those who have become addicted to drugs to stop being buyers in an illegal market and to become patients of the health care system.

Thanks in part to the attention received by our 2009 report, the Latin American Commission evolved into a Global Commission on Drug Policy. This Commission has produced numerous papers and two main reports in 2011 and 2014. With a view to another Special Session of the General Assembly of the United Nations on the world drug problem due to take place in April 2016, the Global Commission, in its latest report of 2014, tried to be bolder in its recommendations. Among various key proposals, we have called for an end to the criminalisation of drug use. However, being aware that decriminalising consumption without taking away from organised crime the provision of the supply of drugs would be counterproductive, even disastrous, we also proposed to reform the global drug policy regime so that governments can intelligently regulate drug markets. As we put it frankly: 'Ultimately this is a choice between control in the hands of governments or gangsters ...'

> 'Ultimately this is a choice between control in the hands of governments or gangsters ...'

Unfortunately, it is practically certain that the Global Commission's aspiration that the 2016 UNGASS be taken as 'an unprecedented opportunity to review and re-direct national drug control policies and the future of the global drug control regime' will be totally disappointed, or so it seems as the preparatory process to the Special Session stands towards the end of 2015.

It is tempting to say – paraphrasing the great Gabriel García Márquez – that the preparatory process of UNGASS 2016 has become *a chronicle of a failure-to-reform foretold*, if for no other reason than that the United Nations entities most invested in preserving the status quo are the ones conducting the preparatory process. In diplomatic parlance, Vienna rather than New York will rule, meaning that the United Nations Commission on Narcotic Drugs (CND) and the United Nations Office on Drugs and Crime (UNODC) – both domiciled in Vienna – have been allowed to take over the negotiation and elaboration of the text that would be approved at UNGASS 2016.

Of course, the fact that the preparatory process was placed on to this track of safe failure is not to be blamed on the secondary layers of UN bureaucracy. It simply reflects that countries opposed to serious reform have used their influence to predetermine their desired outcome. Significant responsibility for this derailment of the needed reform process is also to be found in the governments that, having with good reason sought a change in the international framework for drug policy by promoting UNGASS 2016, have disturbingly become rather passive – and even doubtful about the very need for reform – during the preparation process. Regrettably, this certainly applies to the group of Latin American governments, not least that of my own country, that, having championed a change of approach, have now shrunk their reformist initiative.

Consequently, as I write these notes, I feel tempted to predict that unless a dramatic shift occurs in the early months of 2016 the April UNGASS, apart from using more compassionate and less hawkish language than that used in the past, far from starting a reform of the UN Drug Conventions, will instead reaffirm that these infamous instruments shall continue to be the cornerstone of international drug control policy. It will also reiterate the fallacious consideration that there is sufficient flexibility within those Conventions to accommodate national and regional drug policies.

As the Global Commission and other sources (including the UNODC) have pointed out, it is possible to interpret the Conventions as allowing the decriminalisation of drug consumption. However, as carefully analysed by the experts of the Transform Drug Policy Foundation:

It is also important to note that, while exploration of these less punitive approaches to personal possession and use is allowed within the international legal framework, no form of legal production and supply of any drug prohibited under the conventions, or domestic law, can be explored for non-medical use in any way. The medical prescription model is the only real quasi-exception to this rigid rule; as such, it exists as an island of regulated production and supply, albeit within very narrow parameters. Beyond this there is zero flexibility for any regulated production and supply models to be piloted, tested, researched or explored. Furthermore, this absolute legal barrier creates genuine political obstacles to even discussing or proffering such policy alternatives …

This means that governments could conceivably decriminalise demand without being able to regulate the supply that would satisfy that demand, if they want to operate within the Conventions. But, obviously, it would be inconsistent to decriminalise demand without taking supply out of the hands of criminal organisations. Other aspects being equal, demand liberalisation would boost the illegal traffickers' revenues and thus their criminal power. Ironically, on this topic Nixon (as quoted above) was right: something should not be half legal and half illegal. The problem is that he decided to make that particular something fully illegal rather than legal.

It is a disturbing fact that authorities that have moved their drug policies in the direction suggested by sound knowledge and experience must do it in violation of the international legal framework. Hence the urgency to reform this framework so that countries clearly find within it the policy space to pursue strategies that were vociferously called for in 2014 by the Global Commission: put health and community safety first by moving from failed punitive enforcement to proven health and social interventions; stop criminalising people for drug use and possession; allow and encourage diverse experiments in legally regulating markets in currently illicit drugs, beginning with but not limited to cannabis, coca leaf and certain novel psychoactive substances; and focus on reducing the power of criminal organisations as well as the violence and insecurity that result from their competition with both one another and the state.

If UNGASS 2016 denies the creation of that policy space – as, sadly, it seems will happen – enlightened governments should keep looking for it somewhere else. The stakes are too high to wait 18 years for another United Nations Special Session to start seriously fixing the blatant failure of civilisation that drug policy has been for more than a century.

The stakes are too high to wait 18 years for another United Nations Special Session to start seriously fixing the blatant failure of civilisation that drug policy has been for more than a century

George Soros

George Soros is the founder and chair of Soros Fund Management and the Open Society Foundations. Born in Budapest in 1930, he survived the Nazi occupation during the Second World War and fled Communist-dominated Hungary in 1947 for England, where he graduated from the London School of Economics and Political Science. He then settled in the United States, where he accumulated a large fortune through the international investment fund he founded and managed.

Soros has been active as a philanthropist since 1979, when he began providing funds to help black students attend Cape Town University in apartheid South Africa. The Open Society Foundations today operate in more than 100 countries, with annual expenditures that reached $827 million in 2014, working to promote the values of open society, human rights and transparency.

Soros is the author of more than a dozen books, including *The Tragedy of the European Union* (2014). His articles and essays on politics, society and economics regularly appear in major newspapers and magazines around the world.

Ending the Harms and Irrationality of the Pursuit of a 'Drug-free World'

· · · · · · · · · · · · · · · · · ·

By George Soros

It is a sad irony that aggressive drug policing and harsh drug laws are often justified by policy-makers on public health and security grounds. Basic economic theory tells us that the criminalisation of mood-altering drugs, combined with overemphasis on supply control strategies, dramatically increases the price of these drugs without significantly reducing production or consumption. Criminalisation inevitably favours market participants who are expert in violence, intimidation and corruption. Decades of relying disproportionately on prohibitions and on security and criminal justice institutions to control drugs have profoundly undermined health and security, yielding few successes and extraordinary failures.

> The criminalisation of mood-altering drugs, combined with overemphasis on supply control strategies, dramatically increases the price of these drugs without significantly reducing production or consumption

Growing numbers of countries, states and cities are recognising that this way of doing business is neither morally nor fiscally responsible. It is long past time for new thinking on how psychoactive drugs are addressed by societies.

It is no wonder that Latin American leaders have led the call for a new debate on drugs, which was the impetus for advancing the date of the UN General Assembly Special Session (UNGASS) on drug policy to April 2016. Their countries have borne the brunt of the crime, corruption and violence that is inevitable when organised

Individual successes in reducing drug production or trafficking in one country have merely stimulated production and trafficking elsewhere

criminal networks defend their illegal markets against heavily armed police. Individual successes in reducing drug production or trafficking in one country have merely stimulated production and trafficking elsewhere. Repression of coca production in Bolivia and Peru during the 1990s shifted production to Colombia. Law enforcement successes in Colombia shifted trafficking to Mexico. Now Central American and Caribbean nations are the victims of repressive efforts in Mexico and elsewhere. Far from experiencing greater security, these regions have instead seen spikes in violent homicide that are historically unprecedented in peacetime.

Criminalisation of drug use, minor possession and petty sale has filled prisons in many countries with non-violent offenders who are often the easiest targets for police needing to meet arrest quotas. But there is no evidence that the large-scale arrest and incarceration of

Drug law enforcement has been a ready tool for contributing to entrenched discrimination against already marginalised people

such persons deters drug use or sales. Instead, the burden of criminal records on enormous numbers of people undermines opportunity and needless incarceration eats up public budgets.

Drug law enforcement has been a ready tool for contributing to entrenched discrimination against already marginalised people. The best-documented (but not the only) case is the striking racial disparity at all stages of US drug law enforcement, from stop and search to arrest, detention, sentencing and incarceration. Though rates of illegal drug use and selling are roughly equal across populations groups, African Americans and Hispanic Americans are dramatically over-represented in prisons, including for drug convictions. According to US Department of Justice statistics from 2012, 1 in 13 African American men were in federal or state prison, 1 in 36 Hispanic men and 1 in 90 white men. African American women were incarcerated at a rate 2.5 times that of white women. The consequences for families and communities of people of colour are devastating. In the US, a felony conviction in most states means being ineligible to vote or to receive government benefits or student loans.

This racial disparity is the legacy of a long history of discriminatory policies. The principal motivation for criminalising cannabis passed by US states in the first part of the twentieth century was prejudice against African Americans, Mexican Americans and Mexican immigrants who were portrayed in the press as being addicted to 'killer weed'. African Americans and Latinos use cannabis at similar rates to white people, but Latinos and especially African Americans are arrested at hugely disproportionate rates in most US jurisdictions. As for cocaine, in the US the vast majority of people arrested for crack cocaine offences are African American, even though the majority of people who use it are white. Until 2010 federal sentences for crack cocaine infractions were 100 times more severe than for powdered cocaine – used mostly by whites – though the substances are largely the same. A 2010 law modified the disparity to about 18 to 1, an improvement but still a problem and still irrational. In Canada and Australia, aboriginal people have also faced disparate treatment in drug law enforcement. Discriminatory application of criminal law on drugs is a fundamental corruption of what should be one of society's most important tools for protecting the public.

The criminalisation of cannabis did not prevent its becoming the most widely used illegal substance in the United States and many other countries, but it certainly resulted in extensive costs and negative consequences. Law enforcement agencies today spend

> **Removing cannabis from illegal markets in the Americas would undoubtedly cut into the power of some traffickers**

billions of taxpayer dollars annually trying to enforce this unenforceable prohibition. In the US the 600,000+ arrests made each year for possession of small amounts of cannabis represent more than 40 per cent of all drug arrests. One estimate suggests that Mexican drug trafficking organisations get revenue of about $2 billion a year from cannabis, almost as much as their take from cocaine. While drug traffickers may be able to adapt and compensate with other illegal activities, removing cannabis from illegal markets in the Americas would undoubtedly cut into the power of some traffickers.

Health services and social support neglected

All political leaders are in favour of preventing young people's drug use and involvement in drug markets, but few countries invest in programmes that address the realities that affect young people's decision-making on drugs. The United States, for example, has spent billions in public funds for programmes that attempt to scare young people about the dangers of drugs or to portray all drug use as a moral failure, but these programmes have not reduced or delayed drug use among youth. Funding such programmes is certainly easier than dealing with poverty, unemployment, discrimination and other factors that may underlie drug market involvement. Moreover, programmes based on the goal of complete lifetime abstinence from drugs do not help young people understand drug-related harms and how to use drugs as safely as possible.

Only a relatively small percentage of people who use psychoactive drugs develop problems, but those who do should have access to humane and scientifically sound treatment and support. In many countries, however, treatment for drug dependence is completely unregulated and often left to the private sector or government security sectors, which use beatings, forced labour and other punitive methods as part of 'treatment'. In some countries minor offenders may be detained in compulsory rehabilitation centres in the name of treatment even if they are not drug-dependent. Few countries ensure monitoring of the quality of drug treatment, and very few have functioning mechanisms of complaint and redress for those whose rights are abused in the name of treatment.

While sexual and mother-to-child transmission of HIV has declined, HIV epidemics linked to injection with contaminated equipment continue to grow in a number of countries. Investment in HIV prevention measures such as ensuring access to sterile injection equipment is opposed politically in many places. Opponents argue that needle and syringe programmes encourage drug

HIV epidemics linked to injection with contaminated equipment continue to grow in a number of countries

use, but extensive evaluations by the World Health Organization (WHO) and others demonstrate that this is not the case. The fastest-growing HIV epidemics of any region are in Eastern Europe and Central Asia where HIV transmission linked to injection is prominent. In the Russian Federation, hundreds of thousands of people inject heroin but access to effective and cost-effective opioid maintenance therapies is banned. In some countries with large numbers of people who inject drugs such as Russia, China, Ukraine and Malaysia, coverage of HIV and viral hepatitis treatment is low. Misinformed and discriminatory policies exclude people who use drugs from medical care; they are neither seen to be worthy of costly therapies, nor are they thought to have the capacity to adhere to treatment protocols, in spite of evidence to the contrary.

Women who are drug dependent rarely have access to the kind of care they need. As the principal caregivers of children in most societies, they face a double stigma as drug users and 'unfit parents' and often have to fight to keep custody of their children. Services for treating drug dependence are often designed for men, though women tend to initiate drug use under different circumstances from those of men and also have different physiological reactions to drugs.

Turning a new page

The convening of UN Member States around drug control issues in April 2016 comes at a time when public opinion and the inclinations of political leaders in some countries are shifting away from punitive approaches. The regulated legal markets for cannabis in several US states and nationally in Uruguay represent pioneering steps away from criminalisation-based policy. These jurisdictions as well as countries in Western Europe and elsewhere that have effectively decriminalised minor drug offences have for the most part had healthy debates about the wastefulness of having police chase after minor offenders and filling prisons with those who are not a threat to society. They have considered whether the easy access to cannabis and other substances that young people often have in illegal markets can be better restricted and monitored in a regulated legal market.

> The regulated legal markets for cannabis in several US states and nationally in Uruguay represent pioneering steps away from criminalisation-based policy

Latin American countries are confronting the US over prohibitionist approaches and the violence and insecurity they bring. The decision of Colombia in 2015 to stop aerial herbicide spraying of coca fields in spite of US support for the activity challenges a long-standing status quo. Sitting heads of state in the region have advocated openly for at least exploring policies that reject the 'zero tolerance' spirit of prohibition, a position that was politically unthinkable for a long time.

A number of European countries have essentially eliminated HIV transmission linked to drug injection as a public health problem. They have ensured ready access to clean injection equipment and in some cases have established supervised injection sites where people can inject illegal drugs in the presence of health-care professionals in case they experience overdose or other problems. Opioid overdose is being addressed more widely as many countries are beginning to remove legal barriers to putting naloxone – a medicine that reverses opioid overdose – in the hands not only of emergency medical teams and police but also of drug users and their families. Some countries have made opioid maintenance therapy and even needle and syringe programmes available in prison as well as in the community.

Lower-income countries are also finding their way to good practices, even if the letter of the law is unchanged. In Tanzania, for example, which has harsh drug laws and a high prevalence of heroin injection especially along its Indian Ocean coastline, a pioneering methadone therapy programme has helped people so convincingly that the police in some cases steer people to treatment sites rather than locking them up. Local NGOs help patients with transportation to the treatment facilities and help communities understand the importance of humane care for people who inject drugs. In a number of countries, community groups have worked with the police to stop practices that undermine access to health services. In Kolkata, India, for example, police frustrated by arresting the same people again and again have worked with communities to

> In a number of countries, community groups have worked with the police to stop practices that undermine access to health services

establish drop-in centres where people who use drugs can be referred to essential services and support.

The cannabis legalisation experiences in the US and Uruguay provide an opportunity for learning best practices in government regulation of drug markets. Mistakes will no doubt be made along the way, and it is essential that objective scientific research be brought to bear in evaluating costs and benefits of the new approaches. It already seems clear that taxpayers in Colorado, the first US state to implement regulated legal cannabis, have simultaneously saved substantial public monies in enforcement and incarceration costs and benefited from new revenues from cannabis taxation. Police who would otherwise chase after minor cannabis offenders are freed up to focus on serious crime.

In October 2015 the US government announced that it would begin to release what may eventually be over 40,000 people serving sentences for minor drug offences in federal prisons. This development results from the realisation that federal mandatory minimum sentences for relatively minor infractions were unjust and did not serve to deter drug-related crime. Similar initiatives are needed in the 50 state prison systems in which the majority of US prisoners are held, not to mention systemic reforms that drastically reduce the senseless severity of current sentencing policies.

Reclaiming the global debate

unfortunately political forces are strongly in favour of maintaining the status quo, and some political leaders will perpetuate a 'tough on drugs' posture whether or not it makes sense. UN debates are not the last word, but the UNGASS on drug policy could help by rejecting the prohibition paradigm and showing leadership in a sensible discussion on drugs for the twenty-first century. There should be a frank recognition of the failures of harsh policing and overreaching criminalisation and a welcoming of new approaches and objective research to evaluate them. Where regulated legal drug markets are not politically possible there should at least be decriminalisation of drug use, minor possession and petty sales. Incarceration and pre-trial detention should be rejected as first-line responses to minor infractions. Health and social support services must be made available to all who need them, including appropriate support for women. Needle and syringe programmes, opioid maintenance therapy and programmes to prevent and reverse overdose are cost-effective and life-saving and should be made readily available to all. Well-informed education about drugs for young people, including how to protect themselves from drug-related harm, is an essential investment that pays for itself.

Reducing the harm of criminalisation and the demand for illegal drugs are not incompatible – quite the contrary. And both can guide policies that are consistent with the bedrock UN ideals of human rights and justice as well as with good public policy and public health practice. For too long ideology and 'tough on crime' posturing have dominated global and national drug policy debates. It is time to be humble about the mistakes of the past and to embrace a rational and responsible policy on drugs.

> Health and social support services must be made available to all who need them, including appropriate support for women

> Well-informed education about drugs for young people, including how to protect themselves from drug-related harm, is an essential investment that pays for itself

Ruth Dreifuss

Ruth Dreifuss served as president of the Swiss Confederation in 1999. She studied social work and later economics at the University of Geneva, and gained experience in journalism, psychiatry and international development cooperation. A leader of the federation of labour unions, she was elected as one of the seven members of Switzerland's federal government. As Head of the Department of Home Affairs from 1993 to 2002, her responsibilities included, among others, public health, scientific research and social security. Since her retirement from political office she has been active in the fields of public health and intellectual property, abolition of the death penalty and drug policy.

Killing for the Sake of 'Health and Welfare'

· · · · · · · · · · ·

By Ruth Dreifuss

The global drug control regime, enshrined in three international conventions, pretends to align all states behind the aim of promoting *health and welfare for mankind*. But the repressive and harmful nature of the policies implementing these conventions is a far cry from realising this noble objective.

By focusing on the prohibition of production, sale and consumption of a growing list of psychoactive substances, and by criminalising the whole chain of the drug market, most governments fail to consider the impact the resulting constant fear of punishment has on access to medical and social support. They ignore the fact that forcing people to consume drugs in hiding leads to unsafe use – unsafe for the consumer, but also for society through the spread of transmissible diseases. They also chase the mirage that, through the harassment of consumers, dealers, drug mules and farmers, those leading the criminal organisations in control of the global drug trade can be neutralised. They cannot.

> Forcing people to consume drugs in hiding leads to unsafe use – unsafe for the consumer, but also for society through the spread of transmissible diseases

Repression: the standard response

Ever since the first Single Convention on Narcotic Drugs was adopted in 1961, the standard response to the steady increase in drug supply and demand has been yet more repression. This trend was reinforced after the adoption of the 1988 Convention Against Illicit Traffic in Narcotic Drugs and Psychotropic Substances, which required that 'each Party shall … establish as criminal offences' all activities prohibited under the international regime.

The Conventions require that in addition to production and trafficking, all preparation activities (possession, purchase and cultivation) must also be established as criminal offences – unless it would be unconstitutional or contrary to basic concepts of the country's legal system. In other words, respect for the most basic principles, guaranteeing the fundamental rights of the person, are left to national discretion – 40 years after the adoption of the UN Universal Declaration of Human Rights!

The UN conventions do allow Member States also to add measures such as treatment, education, aftercare, rehabilitation or social integration to their responses, or, in the case of a minor offence, to *replace* conviction or punishment entirely with them.

However, the conventions give far greater weight to punishment and criminal sanction, while medical and social interventions are only described as secondary alternatives to law enforcement. This prioritisation was translated into most domestic laws and practices, until the death toll became so high, and the negative impacts on communities so obvious, that at least in some countries political shifts towards public health had to be undertaken.

And yet millions of people – most of them non-violent offenders – are still incarcerated for offences against national drug laws. Thousands suffering from addiction are detained in compulsory 'treatment' centres

The death toll became so high, and the negative impacts on communities so obvious, that at least in some countries political shifts towards public health had to be undertaken

without their consent. Bearing the stigma of a criminal record, often rejected by society, and at great risk of relapsing, many of them will endure a 'social death'.

One of the most appalling examples of the link between drug policy and mass incarceration is the United States of America: the prison population has roughly doubled every 20 years, from a quarter of a million in 1975 to over one million in 1995 and over two million in 2015. A large proportion of those in prison were sentenced for drug-related crimes, including possession, under a regime of mandatory minimum sentences that doesn't give judges any choice other than to impose lengthy prison terms.

The cruelty and inefficacy of mass incarceration and long detention is becoming increasingly obvious. As a result, the criminalisation of drug users and the proportionality of sentencing for drug crimes are – rightly – progressively influencing the global drug policy debate.

> A large proportion of those in prison were sentenced for drug-related crimes, including possession, under a regime of mandatory minimum sentences that doesn't give judges any choice other than to impose lengthy prison terms

UN-backed decriminalisation to the fore

A broad spectrum of UN bodies including the World Health Organization (WHO), UNICEF, UNAIDS, UN Development Programme and many more have now recommended decriminalising drug users. The United Nations Office on Drugs and Crime (UNODC) has expressed similar views, namely in reports on the prevention of the HIV/AIDS and Hepatitis C epidemics. In October 2015 a briefing paper drafted by the UNODC even called for Member States to renounce punishment for drug use and possession for personal consumption. In fact, the paper went a step further, recommending that 'small drug-related offences', such as drug dealing to maintain personal drug use or to survive in a very marginalised environment, could be interpreted as 'cases of a minor nature' and so 'should receive rehabilitation opportunities, social support and care, and not punishment'. At the time of writing, the paper has not been formally adopted, but it underlines that the direction of travel is towards reform.

In the same spirit, and following a reform of its criminal laws, Ecuador has in recent months freed thousands of 'drug mules' – women who had been arrested for smuggling small quantities of cocaine.

Sadly, though, the reality in some countries is far from Ecuador's wisdom and compassion. Perhaps the worst consequence of failed drug policies is that thousands of people are dying not through the violence of the drug wars, not from overdoses and lack of harm-reduction services, and not as 'unintended casualties' of the War on Drugs. They are dying because they were sentenced to death by a court, killed in the name of the state – in cold blood and often after agonising months or years on death row.

Imposition of the death penalty for drug offenders has followed the same trends as incarceration rates: the estimated number of countries with capital punishment for drug offences in their criminal laws increased from 10 in 1979, to 22 in 1985, and to 33 in 2012.

In 2015 Indonesia executed 14 people by firing squad for drug offences, after a four-year moratorium on executions. Saudi Arabia executed at least 175 people in the last 12 months alone, almost a third of whom were accused of drug-related offences. And of the nearly 700 people executed in Iran in the first seven months of 2015, 80 per cent are estimated to have been drug-related offenders.

At least 13 countries, including China and Malaysia, impose mandatory death sentences for drug-related offences. As a result, judges have no discretion to consider the facts of a given case or individual characteristics of offenders. And thousands of people languish on death row for drug-related crimes across Asia, Africa and the Middle East.

All these tragedies are occurring despite the fact that the death penalty demonstrably fails to deter crime, drug-related or otherwise. Executions for drug offences simply do not lead to significant shifts in either supply or demand. On the contrary, the drug trade is resilient to the threat of capital punishment, partly because the illicit market is far too lucrative, and partly because most of those executed are 'little fish' exploited by criminal organisations that have no difficulty in replacing them.

> All these tragedies are occurring despite the fact that the death penalty demonstrably fails to deter crime, drug-related or otherwise. Executions for drug offences simply do not lead to significant shifts in either supply or demand

Growing movement against capital punishment: the right to life

There is, however, a growing global movement opposing the use of capital punishment for drug-related offences, and retaining it now runs counter to the momentum building for its abolition for all crimes.

According to the United Nations, some 160 countries have abolished capital punishment, whether *de jure* or *de facto*. In December 2014, 117 UN Member States voted in favour of a UN resolution calling for a worldwide moratorium. And 81 States have ratified the Second Optional Protocol to the International Covenant on Civil and Political

Rights, committing them to prevent executions within their jurisdiction and take all necessary measures to abolish the death penalty. The International Covenant also states that where countries do retain the option of capital punishment, then it has to be reserved for only the 'most serious crimes'.

The UN Human Rights Council consistently urges governments to abolish capital punishment for drug offences, noting that they do not fall within the category of most serious crimes. More recently, the International Narcotics Control Board (INCB) has for the first time called on Member States to adopt international standards concerning the prohibition of the death penalty for drug-related offences.

Civil society groups active at local and national levels, international non-governmental organisations such as Amnesty International, and Human Rights Watch are advocating change, with countries that execute drug offenders routinely denounced for committing human rights violations and imposing disproportionate punishment.

It is vital to refute the claims of some death penalty retentionist states that the international drug conventions allow laws and practices that are banned by fundamental human rights instruments. UNODC must also end its 'technical support' for counter-narcotics operations when there is a risk of the organisation becoming an accomplice in executions.

Capital punishment for drug-related offences should be suspended all over the world, and there are both opportunities and pressures for countries retaining capital punishment to change course

In short, capital punishment for drug-related offences should be suspended all over the world, and there are both opportunities and pressures for countries retaining capital punishment to change course.

Enlightened decision-makers can – and do – demonstrate courage and leadership by resisting populist temptations, and deciding in favour of recognising the most important of all human rights, the right to life. Vietnam recently announced an end to the death sentence for seven offences, including drug possession, but does retain it for some other drug offences. A more modest step is to get rid of the *mandatory* death penalty for drug-related crimes, giving judges the option of other sentences, something that Malaysia may soon be ready to do.

From the United Nations General Assembly Special Session on drug policy in 2016, to the establishment of a new ten-year international drugs strategy in 2019, the next few years will provide great opportunities to call on all states to abolish the death penalty for drug offences, or at least to agree to a moratorium. This period is also a chance to comprehensively review, assess and evaluate current drug control measures on a global level, and to honestly recognise the failure of the punitive approach. This would clear the path to introduce greater proportionality, foster better social integration, end discrimination and uphold respect for universal human rights.

> The next few years will provide great opportunities to call on all states to abolish the death penalty for drug offences, or at least to agree to a moratorium

Anand Grover

A long-time advocate and activist on HIV and human rights, Anand Grover is a designated Senior Advocate practising in the Supreme Court of India. He is the Director of the Lawyers Collective. From 2008 to 2014 he served as the UN Special Rapporteur on the Right to Health.

He is presently a member of Global Commission on Drug Policy and a member of the Lancet-University of Oslo Panel on Global Governance of Health.

The War on Drugs: A Violation of Human Rights

• • • • • • • • • • • •

By Anand Grover

As a direct consequence of the War on Drugs, more than half of those incarcerated in prisons in many parts of the world are there for drug-related offences, including possession and consumption. Given that this is just one of the many negative consequences of the global drug war, we must ask: has it succeeded in its objective of eradicating non-medical drug use and made the world drug-free, and are the costs that have been paid by ordinary people worth it?

More than half of those incarcerated in prisons in many parts of the world are there for drug-related offences, including possession and consumption

The use of drugs in history and in context

To answer these questions it is necessary to reflect on the history and context of drug use. Traditionally, drugs have been used for medical, religious or cultural purposes all over the world. Opium was used for medicinal purposes across Asia, from Persia to China to Indonesia. In Persia, Avicenna's treatise, *Canon on Medicines*, discusses the therapeutic uses of opium extensively. Smoking it with tobacco, as *madhak,* became common in China, particularly in ritualistic and social gatherings.

Cannabis, too, has been used for hundreds of years in Asia, particularly in India, where it has been described as a 'way of life', as well as being a medicine in indigenous medical systems. *Kratom* has been used traditionally in Thailand and Malaysia for medicinal, cultural and other purposes. Similar cultural practices existed in South America among native communities, particularly with regard to coca. Alcohol and tobacco, also drugs, of course, have been traditionally used for recreational and cultural purposes, originally in the West and now all over the world.

This all changed with the three UN Drug Conventions of 1961, 1971 and 1988 which required signatory countries to regulate the cultivation, production, possession, use, transportation and consumption of all listed drugs. Any unauthorised activities, meaning outside of 'medical and scientific use', were mandated to be criminalised. As a result, many states imposed severe penalties for illegal drug-related activities.

The origin of this lies in nineteenth-century notions among moral and evangelical groups about the use of opium and cannabis in the colonies, and whose lobbying culminated in universal drug prohibition. This was despite the findings of the Opium and Hemp Commissions in the late nineteenth century, that the 'mild and moderate use of these substances is not deleterious to health'.

It is ironic that countries in Europe and North America are now 'discovering' the medical uses of cannabis, and changing their laws accordingly, whereas cannabis-related traditional medical practices in Asia and Latin America remain lost

The prejudice of westerners against local practices was so strong that the therapeutic benefits of cannabis were not acknowledged in modern medicine for many years, and are still not in some countries. These prejudices have even been adopted by societies in Asia and Latin America. It is ironic that countries in Europe and North America are now 'discovering' the medical uses of cannabis, and changing their laws accordingly, whereas cannabis-related traditional medical practices in Asia and Latin America remain lost and banned by establishments and governments there.

In short, for societies around the world which had traditional use of these drugs drug prohibition is a 'historical wrong' which needs to be corrected.

Importantly, all three Drug Conventions recognise that their primary objective is protecting the *health and welfare of humankind*. Clearly, therefore, the success of the laws, policies and practices adopted domestically pursuant to these Conventions should be judged on health and human well-being indices. Unfortunately, the evaluation of drug policies is instead done on the basis of enforcement measures – the number of seizures, persons arrested and convicted, etc., with the ultimate goal of making the world 'drug free', rather than maximising health and well-being.

However, while globally seizures of drugs, arrests and imprisonment have only increased over the years, illegal drug manufacture and use have, too. For example, world opium production doubled every decade from 1,200 tons in 1971, to 2,600 tons in 1987, 4,800 tons in 1997 and 9,000 tons in 2007; while production in Afghanistan, which supplies over 90 per cent of the world's illicit opium, reached record levels in 2013. The inevitable – and obvious – conclusion is that prohibitionist drug laws, policies and practices have failed to achieve their objective of a drug-free world.

> While globally seizures of drugs, arrests and imprisonment have only increased over the years, illegal drug manufacture and use have, too

According to some authors, the failure of this War on Drugs strategy is inevitable because it ignores the fundamental market dynamics involved in prohibiting drug production, against a backdrop of well-established and increasing demand.

This view argues that since the eighteenth century opium has been transformed from a luxury to a major global commodity, similar to other drugs such as coffee, tea, tobacco and alcohol.

Drug enforcement in one region just leads to the emergence of production and supply in other regions

In market terms, suppression of supply without reducing this demand pushes up prices, increasing the incentives for criminals to enter the market, until production is once again meeting demand. This drives what the UN Office on Drugs and Crime calls the balloon effect. You squeeze one part of a balloon and the air does not vanish; it simply bulges on the other side. Similarly, drug enforcement in one region just leads to the emergence of production and supply in other regions, and to the development of new psychoactive substances, which are proving impossible to control.

Beyond this failure to deliver its stated aim of eliminating drug use, if one were to evaluate the prohibitionist regime in terms of the objectives of the Drug Conventions, rarely the health and welfare of humankind, or the Right to Health, the failure of the War on Drugs is even more pronounced.

The Right to Health is guaranteed under Article 12 of the International Convention of Economic, Social and Cultural Rights, signed and ratified by the vast majority of the world's states. Among other things, it obliges states to make available health facilities, services and goods, with treatment and access to medicines considered the core obligation under the Right to Health.

Some effects of prohibition

However, prohibition has been responsible for much of the trade shifting from opium smoking to injecting heroin, and the consequent transmission of communicable diseases, including HIV and hepatitis B (HBV) and hepatitis C (HCV). Highly processed drugs, such as heroin, are more compact and more easily transported and distributed than opium, with a higher profit margin. As a result, illicit producers and traffickers have a financial incentive to shift the market (and trade routes) to heroin, with leakage into local markets resulting throughout the transport and distribution chain.

In addition, injection is a more efficient route of drug administration because none of the drug is lost as it is when smoked, so users with limited resources, and only able to source opiates from the illicit market, are more likely to use heroin intravenously as a result. This leads to associated criminality, such as stealing to sustain their habit, and sharing needles, with disastrous consequences, including transmission of HIV and hepatitis B and C.

> Prohibition has been responsible for much of the trade shifting from opium smoking to injecting heroin, and the consequent transmission of communicable diseases

Health outcomes can, however, be much improved by promoting and providing evidence-based harm-reduction services. In many developed countries these include opioid substitution therapy (OST) for drug dependence, and needle-syringe exchanges, condoms, or even medically supervised injection facilities, to reduce the risk of transmission of communicable diseases.

Thankfully, albeit because of the HIV epidemic, a number of developing countries, with a significant push from UNAIDS and the Global Fund to fight AIDS, tuberculosis and malaria, have also been able to provide harm-reduction and OST services for injecting drug users (IDUs) in 'safe havens'. However, in most countries these have not been scaled up, and so are not accessible to many people who use drugs. This problem is compounded by the fact that these services exist on the margins of legality. As criminalisation of drug use persists in these countries, drug users are stigmatised, providing a further barrier to their accessing harm-reduction or OST services. As a result, the prevalence of HIV among IDUs is very high in most developing countries.

Furthermore, in some countries the only treatment administered to allegedly drug-dependent people is abstinence – not evidence-based OST.

The vast majority of drug users who pass through such compulsory detention centres return to drug use after the compulsory period of detention and detoxification programmes

This includes the authorities resorting to compulsory detention for treatment, an approach that is flawed for a number of reasons. Firstly, there is no scientific basis for determining if people are drug-dependent, with only urine analyses being used. Consequently, people who are not drug-dependent are forced into compulsory detention centres. Secondly, these 'treatments' are accompanied by punishment, sometimes forced unpaid labour, solitary confinement and experimental treatment without consent. Thirdly, they don't work. The vast majority of drug users who pass through such compulsory detention centres return to drug use after the compulsory period of detention and detoxification programmes. Finally, compulsory drug treatment is in violation of the Right to Health enshrined in Article 12 of the International Covenant on Economic, Social and Cultural Rights.

While many governments across the world felt obliged to introduce harm-reduction and OST services because of the HIV epidemic, with the perceived waning of the epidemic there is a real danger that such services may not be available in the future, particularly to drug users in developing countries. This is being exacerbated by the withdrawal of the Global Fund from middle-income countries, a matter of urgent concern.

The other deleterious consequence of criminalisation of drug use is that millions of people worldwide who require essential medicines, like morphine, for treatment and palliative care are unable to access them. This is a direct consequence of excessively restrictive sanctions instilling fear in the medical community of falling foul of the law. The lack of access is particularly acute in developing countries. While over 90 per cent of all legally controlled medicines is consumed in North America and Europe, 70–90 per cent of patients who require these essential medicines in developing countries do not have access to them.

While HIV has been addressed in the past, HCV, a larger and growing epidemic, has been completely ignored in developing countries. This is because, instead of seeing this disease from the perspective of the person affected and introducing the holistic treatment needed, we have only seen it from the perspective of the disease, in a silo.

The routes of transmission are practically the same as for HIV, but HCV is more transmissible. The prevalence of HCV is over four times higher than HIV. Vulnerable groups, particularly people who use drugs, are often co-infected with HIV, TB and now HCV. As a group, drug users are now the most affected by HCV. It is no coincidence that while the international community was able to mount a response to HIV, there is no such movement on HCV, despite the urgent need to address this epidemic and make testing facilities and treatment available.

Fortunately, with the advent of new and better drugs, HCV is completely curable, within a short period of time. The traditional treatment, to which not all strains respond positively, has been superseded by direct-acting oral antivirals. With a combination of these drugs, all strains of HCV can be cured. However they are prohibitively expensive. For example, Sofosbuvir, one of the antivirals used, is available in the US at $84,000 per treatment.

As previously noted, criminalisation has also resulted in the incarceration of large numbers of people for 'drug-related offences'. Beyond the burden on taxpayers, drug users do not have access to preventative and treatment services (OST), exacerbating the already

Beyond the burden on taxpayers, drug users do not have access to preventative and treatment services (OST), exacerbating the already high prevalence of HCV and HIV among drug users in prisons

high prevalence of HCV and HIV among drug users in prisons.

Another profound and far-reaching impact of criminalisation is in 'impairing and impinging on the dignity of people who use drugs'. Seen as morally depraved and blameworthy, drug users are treated as less than human, undeserving of respect, rights and opportunities. Not only do others (state and society) treat people who use (illegal) drugs with contempt, the individuals may themselves imbibe this sense of unworthiness and denigrate themselves. Nothing can be sadder than this.

Beyond causing mass incarceration, forced detention, increased levels of disease, reduced access to pain relief and the denigration of many millions of people, the prohibitionist regime has also spawned

The prohibitionist regime has also spawned criminal syndicates and gangs who thrive on the exorbitant profits to be made in the illegal drugs market

criminal syndicates and gangs who thrive on the exorbitant profits to be made in the illegal drugs market. In certain countries, particularly those in Latin America, they control vast tracts of land where their writ alone runs. No wonder these same Latin American countries, having had to face the brunt of the War on Drugs, are now seeking change.

In summary, there is no escaping the conclusion that the War on Drugs has failed.

What is the way forward?

First, there must be recognition that the War on Drugs strategy as mandated by the Drug Conventions, and national and international laws to implement them, has failed and has had disastrous consequences for the health and welfare of humankind.

Second, there must be a genuine debate on the issue of drug use in all circles – political, legal and social. Simply saying that all drug use is bad has not been the right approach. Fortunately, the winds of change are blowing. The US, which initiated and led the War on Drugs, is at the forefront of reform, with a number of states having seen the futility of the drug war and legalising the use of cannabis.

Third, people who use drugs must be accorded respect and dignity and treated without discrimination.

Fourth, the response must be based on the primary objective of the Conventions, the health and welfare of humankind, and on the Right to Health framework enshrined in international law.

Taken together, this will mean that:

1. Punitive drug law regimes must be replaced with regulatory measures. If we can do this for alcohol and tobacco there is no reason we cannot, and we should, do this for other drugs as well.

2. Health goods, facilities and services must be available indiscriminately. Preventative and treatment services (including harm-reduction services, OST and essential medicines for palliative care) must be made available and accessible without any discrimination, and with the full informed consent of the proposed recipients.

3. Legal regimes must be tailored to facilitate access to palliative care medicines.

In the era of the HIV epidemic we learned that taking a rights-based approach worked. The key component of that strategy lay in the involvement of the affected communities in the shaping of the response. It is our duty, here and now, to learn what we can, to inform and open a dialogue with our governments to influence them to change policies towards drug use over the crucial coming few years, between the UN General Assembly Special Session on drugs in 2016 to the end of the decade, when a new 10-year international drug strategy will be put in place. We have learned that we can change the world only if we are passionate about our cause and believe in it. We can all do that. And, indeed, we must.

Michel Kazatchkine

Professor Michel Kazatchkine has spent the last 30 years fighting AIDS as a leading physician, researcher, administrator, advocate, policymaker and diplomat. He attended medical school at Necker-Enfants-Malades Hospital in Paris, studied immunology at the Pasteur Institute and completed post-doctoral fellowships at St Mary's Hospital in London and Harvard Medical School.

Professor Kazatchkine served as Director of the National Agency for Research on AIDS (ANRS) in France (1998–2005), and as Chair of the WHO's Strategic and Technical Committee on HIV/AIDS (2004–2007). From 2005 to 2007 he was French Ambassador for the fight against HIV/AIDS and Communicable Diseases. In 2007 he was elected Executive Director of the Global Fund to fight AIDS, tuberculosis and malaria, a position in which he served until March 2012.

In July 2012 Professor Kazatchkine was appointed as the UN Secretary General's Special Envoy on HIV/AIDS in Eastern Europe and Central Asia. He is also a member of the Global Commission on Drug Policy.

From Substance-focused to People-centred Policies: The Central Role of Harm Reduction

· · · · · · · · · · · · · · ·

By Michel Kazatchkine

Unsafe injecting drug use remains a key driver of HIV and hepatitis C epidemics in many countries around the world, particularly in South West Asia, Eastern Europe and Central Asia. HIV transmission through injecting drug use has also recently emerged as a concern in Eastern Africa and other parts of the continent.

HIV and injecting drug users: a present but preventable threat

Rates of HIV infection are high among people who inject drugs, ranging from 10 to over 50 per cent, depending on the country, with additional intra-country variations. It is estimated that the overall risk of HIV infection among people who inject drugs is 22 times greater than in the general population. In addition, most of the approximately two million HIV-infected people who inject drugs also live with hepatitis C infection. In China, the Russian Federation and Vietnam, co-infection rates are more than 90 per cent.

Once HIV is introduced in a group of people who inject drugs and share injection equipment, epidemic outbreaks may surface and expand very quickly. Recent examples include outbreaks of HIV among injecting drug users in Greece and Romania following abrupt decreases in funding for prevention services at the peak of the economic crisis and the withdrawal of donor funding for preventative programmes in the country.

The continued growth of an unsafe injection-linked HIV epidemic globally contrasts with the significant progress that has been seen in reducing sexual and vertical transmission of HIV in the last three decades. In fact, many of the HIV infections that have occurred in the

The continued growth of an unsafe injection-linked HIV epidemic globally contrasts with the significant progress that has been seen in reducing sexual and vertical transmission of HIV in the last three decades

last 30 years through injecting drug use and most of the infections that occur today could have been prevented if the right policies had been in place, starting with large-scale implementation of harm-reduction measures. Many of the other health-related harms associated with injecting drug use, including deaths from overdose, could similarly have been substantially reduced.

Drug policy has not, however, been an area where evidence-base and effectiveness have led the way. Thus, infections with HIV and hepatitis C that have already claimed millions of lives cannot be considered merely as the consequence of 'irresponsible unsafe individual practices'. In many countries across the world, these epidemics, along with tuberculosis and deaths by overdose, have been fuelled by misguided drug policies that prioritise prohibition law enforcement and repression over individual and public health. Based on scientific evidence of effectiveness and on a large body of experience, particularly from Western Europe and Australia, the World Health Organization (WHO), the Joint United Nations Programme on HIV/AIDS (UNAIDS) and the United Nations Office on Drugs and Crime (UNODC) have jointly recommended a package of nine interventions as a harm-reduction approach to injecting drug use. The harm-reduction interventions aim at reducing the risk of acquiring HIV, hepatitis and TB, and improving treatment and care in people who inject drugs.

The first four of these interventions, needle-syringe exchange/ provision programmes (NSP), opioid substitution therapy (OST),

THE COMPREHENSIVE HARM-REDUCTION PACKAGE

1. Needle and syringe programmes (NSPs)

2. Opioid substitution therapy (OST) and other drug-dependence treatment

3. HIV testing and counselling

4. Antiretroviral therapy (ART)

5. Prevention and treatment of sexually transmitted infections

6. Condom programmes for injecting drug users and their sexual partners

7. Targeted information, education and communication for injecting drug users and their sexual partners

8. Vaccination, diagnosis and treatment of viral hepatitis

9. Prevention, diagnosis and treatment of tuberculosis

testing and counselling for HIV and provision of antiretroviral treatment (ART), are the most critical.

There is comprehensive and compelling evidence that NSP and OST are effective in reducing the sharing of injecting equipment and averting HIV infections. In combination with ART, these interventions reduce HIV transmission, decrease mortality, reduce drug dependency, reduce crime and disorder and improve quality of life. Harm-reduction interventions have also been shown to be highly cost-effective in terms of HIV outcomes and reduction of drug dependency from both government and societal perspectives.

Interestingly, mathematical modelling of the impact of these interventions has shown that NSP, OST and ART act synergistically, so that even if the coverage of each of these interventions is below

50 per cent, their synergy can lead to effective prevention of HIV at a community or country level, provided that the three interventions are effectively implemented.

Needle and syringe programmes may consist of needle exchange programmes or those providing sterile injection equipment at specific sites or as mobile and outreach services. Needle and syringe programmes reduce transmission of HIV and other blood-borne viruses, such as hepatitis B and C. At a population level, NSPs appear less effective in preventing hepatitis, which stems, among other reasons, from the fact that people who inject drugs enter an NSP programme after several months or years of previous history of unsafe injections that has resulted in an early infection with the hepatitis viruses prior to entry into a harm-reduction programme. The risk of contracting hepatitis C when sharing injection equipment is significantly higher than for HIV due to the hepatitis virus's greater infectivity and to the fact that the virus survives for some time in needles, syringes, filters and water used for injections.

Community-based outreach is an effective means of getting people who inject drugs who often face barriers to accessing mainstream health services

Needle and syringe programmes are also effective in that they provide a contact with service providers on a regular basis and thus serve as an entry point to health care and social services. Community-based outreach is an effective means of getting people who inject drugs who often face barriers to accessing mainstream health services. Outreach is also highly effective in delivering condoms, information and prevention to people at risk. It is essential that government contract with non-governmental organisations that provide outreach services, as an extension to the conventional health care and social services sector.

The recent decrease in the number of new HIV infections among people who inject drugs in Ukraine, for example, has clearly been associated with the ability of the non-governmental sector to reach out with information and prevention tools to at least two-thirds of the estimated 300,000 injecting drug users in the country. In Estonia, a country with one of the highest rates of HIV in Europe, HIV infections among new injectors decreased from 34 to 16 per cent as the country quadrupled the number of syringes exchanged in the early 2000s.

Opioid substitution therapy (also often referred to as 'medically assisted therapy') is highly effective in reducing injecting behaviours and, consequently, the risk of becoming infected with HIV in people who are dependent on opioids. OST is a proven effective means of treatment for opioid dependence. It has been demonstrated to reduce overdose and overall mortality of dependent users, increase the probability of long-term cessation of opioids and improve health and psychosocial outcomes. OST increases retention in care and compliance with antiretroviral treatment.

Methadone and buprenorphine are the most commonly used opioid agonist agents used for OST. Both are taken orally on a daily basis. Take-home doses can be offered when the dosing of treatment and the social situation of the treated person are stable. Both methadone and buprenorphine are on the WHO list of essential medicines.

Despite the evidence, the response to HIV and hepatitis C related to unsafe injecting and implementation of harm reduction remains poor. Of 158 countries reporting injecting drug use, 90 include needle exchange programmes and 80 include OST in national policy, but only in a few has harm reduction been brought to a sufficient scale to have a significant impact in decreasing HIV transmission. In Eastern Europe and

> Despite the evidence, the response to HIV and hepatitis C related to unsafe injecting and implementation of harm reduction remains poor

Central Asia, where the epidemic is so much associated with unsafe injecting use, less than 8 per cent of people in need of NSP and OST may access harm-reduction programmes.

The epidemiological evidence is clear: in countries that have adopted harm-reduction and health-based approaches to drug use and addiction, the HIV epidemic among people who use drugs has declined, as is the case in most Western European countries where people who inject drugs represent less than 2 per cent of newly diagnosed HIV infections. But in countries and regions that have neglected harm reduction and relied on ineffective and aggressive drug law enforcement, the HIV epidemic is growing fast and worsening. In the Russian Federation or in Thailand, two countries that do not implement harm reduction, these figures reach 45 per cent.

Although they are not yet part of the UN-recommended package of interventions, there is clear evidence that safe injection rooms are effective in preventing infections related to unsafe injections in people who cannot quit injecting. Safe injection rooms have been introduced in Australia, Canada and a number of Western European countries. Switzerland has also added to its set of treatment interventions the possibility of accessing medical heroin treatment for heroin-dependent people who do not respond to or cannot accept OST.

Antiretroviral treatment is now recommended for all people who have been diagnosed with HIV infection. In addition to its remarkable effects in allowing treated people to live a normal life and potentially enjoy a life expectancy close to that of HIV-negative people, ART is also bringing public health benefits by decreasing the transmissibility of HIV at a population level. By drastically reducing the level of virus in the body, ART decreases the risk of transmission of HIV by a treated person. Such population-wide preventative effects of ART have been demonstrated in British Columbia where the HIV epidemic has largely been driven by unsafe injecting drug use.

The world is, however, far from reaching such an impact globally since access to ART for people who inject drugs remains extremely low, below 15 per cent. Many factors contribute to these poor figures, including fear of police and stigma that drive drug users underground, away from prevention services, away from access to care and medical services, and stigma and discrimination still often present within health-care settings, leading to refusal of services, absurd requirements to be drug-free as a condition to treatment, and breaches of confidentiality.

Finally, services for the prevention and treatment of HIV and hepatitis C in the community, including harm reduction and management of overdose, should also be provided to people in prison and other closed settings. People on OST before entering prisons should continue OST while in prison and should be linked back to community-based OST upon release. Globally, there are far too few effective harm-reduction programmes in detention centres at present. Justice and prison authorities should urgently introduce these programmes and expand them to scale, as a public health and human rights imperative.

> Globally, there are far too few effective harm-reduction programmes in detention centres at present. Justice and prison authorities should urgently introduce these programmes and expand them to scale, as a public health and human rights imperative

While harm reduction has traditionally focused on the prevention of infections, it should also include prevention and management of opioid overdose, which is the leading non-HIV-related cause of death among people who inject drugs. An estimated 70,000 people die from overdose each year, yet overdose is preventable and, if witnessed, treatable. OST is the most effective intervention to prevent opioid overdose among heroin-dependent people. Naloxone, a medicine that is also on the WHO list of essential medicines, is highly effective as a short-acting opioid antagonist in the emergency treatment of overdose together with respiratory support. Distribution and availability of naloxone should now be extended to community-based services in addition to health-care facilities. Moldova has recently introduced naloxone in prisons as part of the harm-reduction package delivered by the health department of the Ministry of Justice.

The AIDS epidemic in people who inject drugs, and their sexual partners, continues to be a serious public health emergency that the world is failing to address despite the evidence that harm-reduction strategies are highly effective in preventing HIV infection among people who inject drugs, and despite the evidence that several countries have succeeded in drastically reducing HIV incidence and prevalence among injectors.

In no other disease, and for no more marginalised population, does such wilful blindness to the evidence persist. With the UN General Assembly Special Session on drugs in 2016, the time has come for the international community to acknowledge the evidence, call for and deliver evidence-based harm-reduction strategies of global scale to reduce HIV and hepatitis C infections, and so protect the health of people who use drugs. Anything less will just needlessly extend human suffering.

> The time has come for the international community to acknowledge the evidence, call for and deliver evidence-based harm-reduction strategies of global scale to reduce HIV and hepatitis C infections, and so protect the health of people who use drugs

Fernando Henrique Cardoso

Fernando Henrique Cardoso was President of Brazil from 1995 to 2002. A sociologist by training, he was a long-time professor of sociology and political science at the University of São Paulo and served as president of the International Sociological Association from 1982 to 1986. Upon entering politics, he served as senator and foreign minister before being elected to Brazil's highest office.

He is currently president of the Instituto Fernando Henrique Cardoso in São Paulo and honorary president of the Party of the Brazilian Social Democracy (PSDB). He is a member of The Elders, the Board of Directors of the Club of Madrid and of the Clinton Global Initiative. Among many other appointments, he also served as co-president of the Latin American Commission on Drugs and Democracy (since 2008), and is the president of the Global Commission on Drug Policy.

Latin America: We Have Counted the Costs, Now We Are Ready for Change

By Fernando Henrique Cardoso

Latin America has suffered long and hard under the War on Drugs. Countries in the region produce, consume and serve as transit corridors in the global drug market. This makes them natural targets in a regime that has up until now focused mostly on combating drug supply, not reducing demand. The consequences have been devastating. It is no wonder that the region is one of the most violent on the planet.

Despite consecutive plans and initiatives launched over the past decades, the global and regional drug markets grew. Drug consumption is still on the rise everywhere, in spite of legislation that for years criminalised users. This has thankfully started to change *de facto* or *de jure*, but only in some countries.

> Drug consumption is still on the rise everywhere, in spite of legislation that for years criminalised users

Furthermore, drug cartels and organised crime have been making more money than ever, producing an ever-increasing amount of drugs. Democratic institutions have suffered under the burden of corruption and loss of legitimacy. Illicit gun trade – mainly small arms – is also closely linked to the dynamics of the drug market and helps explain the surge in violence in the region.

Given this scenario, the time is ripe for change. It is no surprise that Latin American countries have been leading the way, both domestically and internationally.

Counting the costs in Latin America

For a start, a third of the world's 450,000 yearly homicides occur in South America, Central America and the Caribbean, but the region is home to less than a tenth of the world's population. In Brazil – the world leader in violent deaths – more than half of the almost 60,000 such victims are said to have some link to the War on Drugs. Most Latin American countries have also seen huge increases in prison populations and systematic violation of human rights. Taken together, there are many ways the War on Drugs has negatively impacted Latin America. Five pressing issues stand out.

Supply

Traditional drug policies have failed in their primary task of reducing the supply of illicit drugs available on international markets. Indeed, anti-drug policies emphasising aerial herbicide spraying ('fumigation'), eradication and crop substitution have made comparatively minor impacts on the cultivation and production of cocaine, heroin and cannabis in Latin America.

Despite the efforts of the US and the international community to support governments of countries such as Bolivia, Colombia and Peru, coca cultivation and cocaine production trends have remained stable over the last decade. The Andean countries are still responsible for nearly 100 per cent of global cocaine production, notwithstanding slight variations in individual countries' production. Indeed, the well-known 'balloon effect' accounts for persistent regional production as counter-narcotics efforts in one location tend to result in drug production moving elsewhere.

> **Herbicide spraying ('fumigation'), eradication and crop substitution have made comparatively minor impacts on the cultivation and production of cocaine, heroin and cannabis in Latin America**

These policies have also exacerbated the vulnerability of marginalised populations. Crop growers in the Andean region come mostly from traditional communities. They were largely left behind in the regional economic boom of the 2000s and took to the illicit market for subsistence. Countries are now experimenting with alternative development approaches to the issue of supply and illicit drug cultivation. However, as long as there is a steady demand for these plants and their derivatives, there will continue to be a supply. The focus must be on promoting comprehensive development, rather than simply substituting illicit crops for those that are licit.

Transit

Owing to their geo-strategic location between North America and Western Europe, most Latin American and Caribbean countries are negatively affected by the transit of illicit drugs. More than 90 per cent of all cocaine consumed in the US comes from Colombia and is transited through Central America and Mexico, creating a need for traffickers to take the risks necessary to move these products from south to north. Counter-narcotics activities in Colombia, Central America and Mexico have resulted in an expansion of trafficking routes through neighbouring countries, greatly increasing the intensity of corruption and possibly exacerbating violence in various sub-regions. 'Successful' policies intended to counter narcotics and

> Counter-narcotics activities in Colombia, Central America and Mexico have resulted in an expansion of trafficking routes through neighbouring countries, greatly increasing the intensity of corruption and possibly exacerbating violence

Ending the War on Drugs

reduce violence in one country can generate negative effects in others, particularly regarding the protection of human rights. This is one of the main reasons why a regional perspective is necessary to gauge real success in drug policy.

Drug consumption

A major failure of international efforts to counter narcotics is in the area of demand reduction. In 2010 between 150 and 300 million people aged 15–64 (3.4–6.6 per cent of the world's population in that age group) are estimated to have used an illicit substance at least once in the previous year. And levels of consumption appear to be rising or stabilising, not declining.

In Latin America, studies by the UN Office on Drugs and Crime (UNODC) reveal that consumption trends for the various categories of drugs have grown steadily. At the very least, current policies have done little to deter the overall consumption of illicit narcotics. Prevention policies and campaigns based on honest education on narcotics and focused harm reduction are not promoted in most countries, despite the clear failure of the 'just say no' approach.

Despite international guarantees that prohibition should not affect access to pain relief and other types of medication, the reality is far different

Also, access to illicit drugs for medicinal and therapeutic use is a major issue in Latin America. Despite international guarantees that prohibition should not affect access to pain relief and other types of medication, the reality is far different. While access to opiate-based medicines is rather stable, medical and therapeutic use of cannabis is not a reality. Brazil only recently regulated access to cannabidiol (an active substance in cannabis that can be extracted and used for medical purposes) but only for minors suffering from intractable epilepsy.

Promotion of human rights

Efforts to counter drug supply, transit and consumption in Latin America have generated collateral damage in terms of corruption, imprisonment and violations of human rights. Prisons and jails in most countries of the region are bursting, often operating at several times their intended capacity.

A study of the relationships between drug legislation and prison populations in Argentina, Bolivia, Brazil, Colombia, Ecuador, Mexico, Peru and Uruguay concluded that the enforcement of severe laws for drug offences resulted in a massive surge of court caseloads, overcrowded prisons and the suffering of tens of thousands of people for (often first-time) small-scale drug offences and simple possession.

The punitive response has resulted in an over-reliance on penalties and repression that often contribute to violations of basic human rights. And as the drug business flourished, organised crime has extended its reach and today constitutes a major threat to state authority and legitimacy, undermining the democratic process and economic growth.

> As the drug business flourished, organised crime has extended its reach and today constitutes a major threat to state authority and legitimacy, undermining the democratic process and economic growth

Violence and crime

Finally, the failed drug war has contributed to Latin America's rise as the most violent region on the planet, measured by levels of homicidal violence and executions, extrajudicial killings, arbitrary detentions and denial of basic health services. Indeed, conflicts over the production and distribution of illicit drugs – including those waged between drug cartels over the transit of drugs, but also those pursued by national governments against organised crime – have been devastating.

Latin America registers the highest youth murder rate in the world, exceeding that of countries and regions at war

Latin America registers the highest youth murder rate in the world, exceeding that of countries and regions at war. The main victims of police brutality are also young black males between 15 and 19 years old who are generally labelled as drug traffickers in the favelas. These trends persist to this day.

The practice of extrajudicial killings, i.e. the killing of individuals by the authorities outside the course of regular judicial proceedings, is alarmingly common. A 2007 UN report on extrajudicial, summary or arbitrary executions in Brazil established that police were frequently killing criminal suspects instead of investigating and arresting them, and that a high number of suspected criminals and bystanders were being killed during brief, large-scale, military-style police operations in favelas.

Mobilisation around the disappearance of 43 students in Iguala, Mexico, in 2014 has garnered attention both nationally and internationally. A year after the suspected massacre, a lot still remains to be uncovered, but the links with the drug trade and public officials are already clear.

The way forward in Latin America and beyond

As members of both the Latin America Commission on Drugs and Democracy, launched in 2008, and the Global Commission on Drug Policy, founded in 2011, we have questioned the very same drug policies we used to endorse. Our concern arose from the immediate and urgent threat to our emerging democracies and the human rights violations perpetuated by the violence and corruption. The War on Drugs approach has failed and we are ready to raise our voices and find a new strategy.

> The War on Drugs approach has failed and we are ready to raise our voices and find a new strategy

In breaking the taboo and speaking openly about these issues, we have opened the global debate and helped make this a mainstream issue. We have also fomented concrete action, witnessing specific legal and policy transformations in countries most affected by this failed war.

Local change

In just a few years a wide array of policy and programming alternatives to the drug control regime – ranging from the decriminalisation of drug use to harm-reduction practices such as substance analysis to the legal regulation of drugs markets – have been put on the table as viable policy options, in some cases for the first time.

There is a clear shift in Latin America towards harm-reduction efforts and decriminalisation in the region. A landmark ruling by Argentina's Supreme Court has for all practical purposes removed criminal penalties for the possession of small amounts of drugs for personal and immediate consumption. Colombia was actually the first country to take this step. A decision by its Constitutional Court in 1994 scrapped penalties for personal use and if someone is found with a quantity greater than that allowed,

> There is a clear shift in Latin America towards harm-reduction efforts and decriminalisation in the region

the burden of showing intent to distribute rests on the state, rather than the user, demonstrating a more effective decriminalisation. And, most recently, Mexico's Supreme Court ruled that four individuals had the right to cultivate and consume cannabis for personal use in the 'free development of the person', a constitutional right.

Change is also imminent in Brazil. One of the Justices of our highest court made a public appeal for clarification of the differentiation between drug users and drug dealers, and discussions on the ruling began in August 2015. A current ambiguity in the law effectively opens opportunities for police corruption and extortion. Civil society hopes the Supreme Court will address the issue, since neither the executive nor the legislative has taken a stand.

Latin America is also home to the first country to have regulated the production, distribution and use of cannabis, Uruguay. In doing so, then-president José Mujica stated that the reform was a human rights issue. Uruguay is paving the way for other countries which recognise that reform is both imminent and necessary.

International reform

Decisions taken in the next few years could very well set the stage for the emergence of a new international drug policy regime, with profound consequences for international cooperation across the continent.

In September 2012, Mexico, Guatemala and Colombia issued a joint declaration to the United Nations (UN) General Assembly asking it to 'exercise its leadership and conduct deep reflection to analyse all available options' and to hold a General Assembly Special Session (UNGASS) on drugs in 2016. In May 2013 the Organisation of American States (OAS) launched two unprecedented reports and opened a debate at its 43rd General Assembly to develop an 'integral policy for the problem of drugs in the Americas'.

With the encouragement of the Global Commission and civil society, other UN agencies have also stepped forward to highlight the shortcomings of the current drug control regime. In June 2015 the United Nations Development Programme launched a critical report, noting that repressive approaches and eradication efforts have disproportionally impacted people who are economically disadvantaged, in addition to causing damage to the environment, which in turn impacts on both cultivators and the community at large. During the UNGASS preparations, UNAIDS has suggested that the international community include public health as a fourth pillar within the global drug control regime. The Office of the High Commissioner on Human Rights also published a report in May 2015, highlighting the negative impacts of drug policy on human rights, particularly within the justice system, in the protection of children and youth, indigenous people's rights and in discriminating against users more generally. Finally, the United Nations University launched a report in November 2015, drawing attention to the need to build principled pluralism through the UNGASS process and making concrete recommendations of possible outcomes.

Latin America cannot be left alone in the preparations for UNGASS. Europe and Africa must also come to the table with best practices and lessons learned in order to have a fully comprehensive debate. There is much to be learned from these regions, including the experiences of Switzerland, Portugal and others. All countries should seize UNGASS as an opportunity to further an honest debate on drug policy, its shortcomings and the ways forward.

Conclusion

Latin American countries have suffered too long and are ready for change. The consequences of the War on Drugs on social and economic development of the region have been dramatic. A paradigm shift is required, away

> A paradigm shift is required, away from the repression of drug users and cultivators and towards harm reduction, education and prevention

from the repression of drug users and cultivators and towards harm reduction, education and prevention. The challenge is to reduce drastically the harm caused by illegal narcotics and its markets to people, societies and public institutions.

We have come to recognise that repressive policies towards drug users and cultivators are firmly rooted in prejudice, fear and ideological visions, rather than in an evidence-based assessment of the realities of drug abuse. This does not mean we should be complacent regarding narcotics and their purveyors. It is a problem, albeit a public health one, not to be dealt with by the criminal justice system. Public funds should accordingly be redirected towards health, education and safety programmes.

Established human and civil rights movements are realising the relevance of the drug reform agenda to Latin America's and other regions' social development. This is already a big advance. The media also has a clear role to play, bringing the debate closer to the people with more comprehensive and balanced stories and coverage that goes beyond the usual narrative of crime and disease. What we need is broader discussion of how to reduce the social harms caused by prohibition and drug abuse.

There is still a long way to go. The current trend towards decriminalisation of possession helps to empower a public health paradigm, but in order to be truly effective in addressing drug abuse it must also be combined with robust prevention and harm-reduction campaigns and the decriminalisation of small-scale cultivators. Yet even then decriminalisation is not the ultimate solution. In order to tackle all the problems related to the current drug issue we need to start allowing and encouraging countries to carefully test models of responsible, legal regulation as a means to undermine the power of organised crime, which thrives on illicit drug trafficking.

The way forward will involve a strategy of reaching out, patiently and persistently, to users and producers, and not continuing to wage a misguided and counterproductive war that makes the users and marginalised communities, rather than the drug lords, the primary victims. The Uruguayan experience as well as that of Colorado and other states in the US is in the vanguard of this movement. Ultimately this is a choice between control by governments or by gangsters; there is no third option in which drug markets can be made to disappear. Latin American countries, faced with the current state of affairs, have been bold enough to face this debate. I hope they will continue to do so for many years to come.

Ultimately this is a choice between control by governments or by gangsters; there is no third option in which drug markets can be made to disappear

César Gaviria

César Gaviria is the former President of Colombia. Elected to Colombia's highest office in 1990, he is known throughout Latin America as a conflict mediator, advocate of democracy, staunch supporter of regional integration and defender of human rights. During his four-year term in office he enacted policies to strengthen democracy, promote peace and reintegrate armed rebels into civilian life. In 1991, through a plebiscite and elected constitutional assembly, Colombia drafted a new, more democratic constitution. Gaviria was elected Secretary General of the Organization of American States in 1994 and re-elected in 1999. He holds a degree in economics from the Universidad de los Andes in Bogotá.

Drugs and Citizen Security in Latin American Cities

. . . .

By César Gaviria

Colombia is on the front line when it comes to drugs and citizen security. Beginning in the 1970s, the country was in the grip of some of the most ruthless drug trafficking organisations in the world. What started out as a relatively modest trade in cocaine ballooned over four decades into a multinational drugs empire spanning every continent. Major cities of Colombia – Bogotá, Cali and Medellín – were synonymous with organised crime.

> What started out as a relatively modest trade in cocaine ballooned over four decades into a multinational drugs empire spanning every continent

Plan Colombia, a counter-narcotics programme, was one of several major militarised initiatives. The perceived success of the plan is highly overstated in relation to the production and trade of cocaine. It was, however, very successful in improving the security of the Colombian people. Cocaine production and trafficking have remained steady and the conclusion of experts is that Plan Colombia had no meaningful impact on the supply of cocaine, with 90 per cent of the cocaine consumed in the United States originating in Colombia. Clearly new approaches were needed.

In 2009, former Presidents Cardoso of Brazil, Zedillo of Mexico and I convened the Latin American Commission on Drugs and Democracy. Our goal was to highlight the pernicious

> The illegal trade in drugs was and still continues to be a threat to democracy across Latin America

relationships between the drug trade, violence and corruption. The illegal trade in drugs was and still continues to be a threat to democracy across Latin America. After carefully reviewing the region's policy environment, we determined that a public debate must be opened to talk about an issue traditionally associated with fear and misinformation.

Our first publication – *Drugs and Democracy: Towards a Paradigm Shift* – highlighted the enormous complexity and controversial nature of the issue. It was clear that the so-called War on Drugs had failed and that efforts to eradicate production and criminalise consumption had virtually no effect on drug production, trafficking or consumption. What we found instead was that the harm generated by drug prohibition was often greater than that caused by drug use. This was especially the case when considering the high levels of corruption, violence and violations of human rights arising from the War on Drugs.

Since then we have witnessed a seismic shift in how drugs and drug policy are discussed. While we have yet to see a comprehensive change in global policy, increasingly the debate now has human rights, safety, health and development at its centre. Although repressive approaches to drug control are still all too common, there is overwhelming evidence that more effective policies and strategies can be implemented. Mobilising this evidence is one of the goals of the Global Commission on Drug Policy, the successor of the Latin American Commission. Since 2011 we have written five high-level reports that demonstrate how drug policies can be improved.

We began by calling for the decriminalisation of all users, small-scale cultivators and others who are low-level participants in the illicit drugs market. We are also calling on governments to redirect their resources from punitive enforcement to interventions that prioritise health and social welfare. We demand that public authorities focus on the real problem, which includes reducing the power of organized crime. We also seek equitable access to controlled medicines and encourage governments to adopt alternatives to incarceration. Finally, we encourage societies to experiment with legally regulated markets of all illicit drugs, beginning with cannabis and coca leaves.

We have a tremendous opportunity to dramatically change the way the world thinks about drug policy. The United Nations General Assembly Special Session (UNGASS) on drugs is coming up in April 2016. This conference represents an opportunity to ask hard questions about global drug policy and take a balanced look at our progress to date. After we sift through all the evidence and consider our record, particularly in Latin America, we must ask whether it was worth it. What has worked? Should we continue down the same path? Is it finally time to look for alternatives? I think the honest answer is yes.

> We have a tremendous opportunity to dramatically change the way the world thinks about drug policy

Latin America traditionally adopted the US model of drug prohibition. But it has also had the courage to explore alternative routes as well. In many states, small amounts of cannabis and other drugs were decriminalised for personal use. Our region is affected in many ways by the US-led War on Drugs. Some countries have been forced – at tremendous social cost – to try to curb the production and transit of drugs to North America, especially Bolivia, Colombia and Peru, but also many countries in Central America, the Caribbean and Mexico. At the same time, many Latin American societies are also increasingly consuming drugs and being criminalised by domestic law enforcement, justice and penal systems.

Latin American cities bear the brunt of repressive drug policy. This is not surprising since more than 85 per cent of Latin Americans live in urban settings. Today, Latin American cities experience homicide rates that are 5 to 50 times higher than cities in North America and Western Europe. Moreover, competing factions that traffic in drugs often control large areas of Latin American cities, with citizens often being caught in the crossfire. This is well documented in Brazil where levels of urban violence are rivalling those of Colombia. In fact, 15 of the 50 most violent cities in the world are now found in Brazil. For its part, Uruguay decided to legalise cannabis in part to reduce rising levels of violence. Indeed, across the continent, from Chile to Mexico, societies are introducing new approaches to drug policy.

Few countries have experienced the negative effects of the War on Drugs to the same extent as my own, Colombia. For three decades we poured resources into fighting drug production and drug trafficking. More than 100,000 lives were lost in the process. But after $9 billion spent on Plan Colombia, it is hard to detect any positive outcomes. Today, Colombia spends close to 6 per cent of its GDP on national security and fields the largest military and police force in the region. Colombians have witnessed significant increases in security spending but very limited results in terms of reducing the flow of drugs to the US The most recent Inter-American Drug Abuse Control Commission (IADACC) report notes that 95 per cent of the cocaine seized in the US can still be traced to Colombia.

Mexico is also exposed to the devastating effects of a military and police-oriented approach to combating drugs. According to some estimates, more than 120,000 people have been murdered there over the past eight years due in large part to competition related to the illegal drug market. Yet the flow of drugs to the US – cocaine, methamphetamine, cannabis and heroin – has not diminished. The violence is equally widespread and ruthless in Central American countries, especially El Salvador, Guatemala and Honduras. The question on the lips of citizens from across the region is whether this failed policy is worth it. Can

> **The question on the lips of citizens from across the region is whether this failed policy is worth it. Can we keep postponing the inevitable: a new approach to drug policy?**

we keep postponing the inevitable: a new approach to drug policy? It appears that Mexicans are finally saying no. A recent decision by the Mexican Supreme Court that accepted the right of four citizens to cultivate and consume cannabis offers a glimmer of hope. It has led Mexican President Peña Nieto to formally call for a debate on the future of drug policy in his country, which will force the federal government to define a clear path towards a harm-reduction approach and encourage the US to continue revising its approach to drug consumption.

Several Latin American presidents are demanding that the US and other countries change their approach to drugs. They are urging them to reinterpret the 1961 United Nations Single Convention on Narcotic Drugs. They are also calling for more evidence of what works and what does not. In Colombia and Mexico, some portion of violence can be attributed to local consumption rather than international trafficking. But the fact is that we do not know. Surveys are often administered by authorities associated with counter-narcotics and they do not focus on these issues. Furthermore, people who consume drugs are stigmatised, and may fear giving honest answers to questions.

If we are to see a genuine reform of global drug policy, we must accept a simple premise: the War on Drugs has failed. The evidence on the ground is clear. And the wider public also agrees: 70 per cent of polled US citizens disapprove of the country´s approach. More than 50 years after the adoption of the Single Convention and 40 years after the declaration of the War on Drugs by the Nixon administration, the situation has gone from bad to worse. The US has the highest rate of drug consumption in the world, despite having some of the harshest penalties in the world. The country spends $40 billion a year on counter-narcotics efforts, and only small change on prevention and treatment. The US has

> Today more than half of all American citizens approve of legalisation of cannabis. There are increasingly few defenders of the status quo

incarcerated more than half a million people for drug-related crimes, which is more than all Western European countries *for all crime*. But the news is not all bad. Citizens in 24 states have regulated medical or recreational cannabis, after losing faith in prohibition. Today more than half of all American citizens approve of legalisation of cannabis. There are increasingly few defenders of the status quo.

We would do well to learn lessons on enlightened drug policy from Western Europe. In many countries there, the focus is on harm reduction and limiting the damage to people who use drugs and to wider society. Their approach is largely successful. It treats consumers and finds ways to engage them in the health and social welfare system. They are not indiscriminately punished or stigmatised. As a result, many countries have witnessed significant declines in interpersonal and self-inflicted violence, and sizeable decreases in the prevalence of HIV/AIDS and hepatitis C. Remarkably, despite more liberal approaches, there has been no significant increase in consumption, nor evidence of increased corruption of public officials.

Across Latin America, we are increasingly convinced that prohibition in the face of rising global demand is counterproductive. Illicit markets generate vast profit margins that sustain the illegal trade and enrich organised crime groups that are responsible for undermining peace and security around the globe. In addition, the War on Drugs threatens public health and safety, undermines human rights, fosters discrimination and wastes billions of dollars of taxpayers' money. The annual global spending on the War on Drugs probably exceeds $100 billion a year. This compares to the revenue of the illicit drug trade, which has been estimated at $320 billion. A cost-benefit analysis of this policy shows that it simply does not add up. For these reasons the Global Commission on Drug Policy is exploring several key pathways to drug policies that do work.

This includes putting people's health and safety first. If we are to reduce the health harms caused by drug use such as overdoses, HIV/AIDS and hepatitis C, we must stop spending on counterproductive drug law enforcement and scale up evidence-based prevention, harm-reduction and treatment measures. Access to controlled medicines is a human right and must be ensured throughout the world. Colombia recently passed a law to this effect, and other countries, with the support of the United Nations, should also encourage access to palliative care and controlled medicines. Medical cannabis should be made available to patients, and national governments should not stand in the way of those who can benefit from treatment.

Rather than fighting a War on Drugs, we must find ways to control and reduce violence. This includes supporting alternatives to incarceration and exploring proportionate sentencing. Our stated goals and performance metrics should be based on how much violence and corruption are reduced over time rather than how many hectares of illicit crops we have eradicated. What is more, the burden of enforcement invariably falls most heavily on the most vulnerable and marginalised members of society – low-income groups, children and young people, women, ethnic minorities and people who use drugs. We must therefore end punitive responses to low-level, non-violent operatives in the illicit drug trade. Only longer-term socio-economic development efforts that improve access to land and jobs, reduce economic inequality and social marginalisation and enhance security can offer people a legitimate exit strategy from the illicit drug trade.

> Our stated goals and performance metrics should be based on how much violence and corruption are reduced over time rather than how many hectares of illicit crops we have eradicated

Making these changes to global drug policy will require sweat and tears. The evolution of an effective, modern international drug control system requires leadership from the United Nations and national governments, building a new consensus founded on core principles that allow and encourage exploration of alternative approaches to prohibition, including legal, regulated markets. UNGASS provides a space in which Member States and UN agencies have an unprecedented opportunity to demonstrate leadership and initiate a meaningful multilateral reform. We will need to be open and flexible for experimentation. UN Member States at UNGASS can and should begin discussing the flexibility of the drug control conventions, recognising that reform might be necessary and that a one-size-fits-all drug policy is inappropriate in the twenty-first century. If policies are to change, we need decisions to be based on evidence and science.

The World Health Organization must play a larger role in the debate and both Member States and the UN Office on Drugs and Crime must take into account its recommendations. We also urge other UN agencies to bring their voices to the debate on specialised issues that are intricately intertwined with drug policy, such as women, sustainable development and human rights. When we began the Latin American Commission, we did not know that the UN General Assembly would address drug policy in 2016. We did, however, feel the urgency of this issue across our hemisphere. Drug control measures cannot take precedence over health, safety, human welfare and well-being any longer. Our countries have suffered enough. The human costs are too high. Too many people have paid the ultimate price of these failed policies. We know the necessary steps that need to be taken. We are ready to act.

> Drug control measures cannot take precedence over health, safety, human welfare and well-being any longer. Our countries have suffered enough. The human costs are too high.

Olusegun Obasanjo

Olusegun Obasanjo served as President of the Federal Republic of Nigeria from 1999 until 2007. Upon leaving office he oversaw the first civilian handover of power in Nigeria from one democratically elected leader to another.

On a regional level, President Obasanjo has played a pivotal role in the regeneration and repositioning of the African Union and has consistently supported the deepening and widening of regional cooperation.

He has at different times served as Chairman of the Group of 77, Chairman of the Commonwealth Heads of Government Meeting, and today serves on the African Progress Panel to monitor and promote Africa's development. He has also served as the UN Secretary General's Special Envoy on the Great Lakes.

President Obasanjo currently chairs the West Africa Commission on Drugs and is a member of the Global Commission on Drug Policy.

Not Just in Transit – The West African Response to Drugs and Drug Trafficking

By Olusegun Obasanjo

'The police arrested me. When we reached *their office, one inspector woman just use her baton to hit me and shouting "drug smoker, idiot, hopeless woman". She use her baton to push me inside the cell as if I am a goat. They did not give me food, they did not give me water. I slept on the floor for three days … before one of my sisters came looking for me.'*

Female drug user interviewed in Nigeria

Drug users from a poor background are all too often treated like this in West Africa. But even money and support from the family can prove not to be sufficient. When my kid cousin developed a drug dependence, I looked for treatment. I could not find anything apart from a psychiatric facility, which did not measure up to international standards on drug treatment. He was in and out of there until he died.

So when Kofi Annan asked me to chair an independent commission on drugs and drug trafficking in West Africa, I agreed, not only because he was the former Secretary General of the United Nations and one simply does not say no to him. But I agreed also because this experience in my family had shown me that drugs touch everyone; and that the problem needs to be addressed urgently in West Africa where we have long elected to pretend that drugs transiting through our region cause harm only in the rich consumer countries. Together we launched the West Africa Commission on Drugs (WACD). (The 11 commissioners come from politics, civil society, health, security and the judiciary from 10 countries in West Africa.)

Drug trafficking in West Africa

Concerning drugs and West Africa, an outside perspective has been dominant. The focus has been on supply reduction, interdiction and security, which matter to European countries – the destination of most drugs trafficked through our region. Much of the collaboration between the European Union and West Africa in tackling cocaine trafficking is funded as development cooperation but directed at transnational organised crime operating in West Africa. This focus has sidelined other, more pressing issues for Africa such as the provision of drug treatment facilities or the infiltration of drug money in politics. Very little attention is given to root causes, the broader impacts on urban and transit zones, and on national economies and governance. Nor is there much of a discussion on how the current system transfers the costs of prohibition on to poorer producer and transit countries. But it is a fact that drug production and trafficking concentrate in fragile, conflict-affected and underdeveloped regions. 22 of the 34 countries which were least likely to achieve the Millennium Development Goals are either drug producers or lie on drug-trafficking routes. West Africa is particularly vulnerable to transnational criminal activity. Borders are porous, coastlines are under-patrolled. Institutions of governance and justice are still quite fragile and vulnerable to penetration by organised crime and drug money. Our countries are used as transhipment points between producers in Latin America and Asia and consumers in Europe and the United States. As the experience from other transit regions shows, drugs do not only pass through a country. They are *Not Just in Transit*, as the Commission emphasises in the title of its report, *Not Just in Transit – Drugs, the State and Society in West Africa*. An Independent Report by the West Africa Commission on Drugs, June 2014. Drugs and drug money invade and undermine societies. The illicit drug trade has played a direct or indirect role in political upheaval in countries such as Guinea-Bissau and Mali. These developments

> West Africa is particularly vulnerable to transnational criminal activity. Borders are porous, coastlines are under-patrolled

threaten to undo economic and social gains in our region. Illegal businesses, often associated with money-laundering schemes, affect formal economies in many ways, including the distortion of markets worsening income inequality, undermining the rule of law and fuelling corruption. Corruption and violence in turn create a hostile environment for legitimate businesses, deterring investment and tourism. Aid and other resources are directed away from development and into police and military enforcement.

We have found that interdiction is improving in the region. However, it is still hindered by limited capacity and resources and sometimes by the interference of the well-connected. In some countries, people in positions of power, the security services and extremist groups compete for the spoils of drug trafficking. We also believe that West Africa's electoral processes are worryingly vulnerable to corruption by drug money. To put the amounts involved in perspective: while, estimated at US $1.25 billion, the annual value of cocaine transiting through West Africa is only a fraction of the US $80–100 billion that the global cocaine market is thought to be worth, this is still significantly more than the annual national budgets of several countries in the region.

However, while the topic of drugs and terrorism draws a lot of media attention, even creating new terms such as 'narco-jihadism', we have found that the links between drug trafficking and local élites are much more important. When groups operate in drug trafficking and terrorism, they are often more 'criminal entrepreneurs' or 'brothers in crime' rather than subscribing to a hard-core ideology. Militarising the response to drug trafficking would therefore only make matters worse. In many ways, Latin America provides an example for West Africa on how *not* to approach the drug challenge. Africa cannot afford to be the new front line in the failed War on Drugs.

Currently, many drug laws in Africa stipulate harsh sentences for drug use and possession. In addition, these laws are often applied disproportionately to the poor, the uneducated and the vulnerable. An informal sample of prisoners held for drug-related offences in Lagos reveals that prisoners were mainly men under 40 years of age, were

> We have found that it is still mostly drug users and small-time dealers who are arrested and imprisoned. The small fry are caught while the big fish swim free

unemployed and had reached only secondary or lower educational levels. Nearly three-fifths of the offenders were sentenced to less than two years, which is hardly consistent with them being hardened traffickers. So we have found that it is still mostly drug users and small-time dealers who are arrested and imprisoned. The small fry are caught while the big fish swim free. I know this from experience. When I was imprisoned for speaking out for democracy and against the military regime, my fellow inmates were small-time dealers, not drug barons. Drugs were readily available and I felt that many became hardened criminals in prison ready to get involved in higher-level drug trafficking.

Drug consumption in West Africa

During the course of the work of the West African Commission on Drugs, we have come to realise that it is not only drug trafficking which is causing major problems in the region but also drug consumption. Drugs have become increasingly available and drug dependency has increased, especially among the young. The data that we have, albeit rather limited, suggest that the use of cannabis is higher than in most other regions of the world and the use of cocaine is by now at levels comparable to Western Europe. But the health systems in the region do not have the means or capacity to offer adequate prevention, treatment or harm-reduction services to drug users.

Drug users are widely discriminated against and marginalised. The prevailing societal perception in our region is that drugs are a social evil. There is a strong moral dimension to this. Cannabis is called 'devil's tobacco' in Ghana, for example. A lot must change in this regard. It has been proved that harm-reduction services work, yet in West Africa only Senegal currently runs a harm-reduction programme. Negative attitudes towards users stand in the way of making rational choices on which policy options are even considered.

> Negative attitudes towards users stand in the way of making rational choices on which policy options are even considered

Regarding prevention, it is still a 'just say no' approach and mass media campaigns, even though we know that it is most important to target those most at risk and to work with peers. And, again, I know this from personal experience. One of my sons was targeted at his private boarding school by peers who were trying to get him to start taking drugs. When I talked to the principal, it turned out that the kids often target the sons of influential or rich people as they hope that, once they start taking drugs, they will finance the supplies of others. Given the pressure from his peers, my solution was to make my son a day pupil so that the influence of the others was balanced with what he experienced at home.

The way forward

The African Union and ECOWAS (the African Community of Economic States) have already sounded the alarm about the growing scale of the threat and the dangers to governance, security and democracy. The current African Union Plan of Action on Drug Control, which runs until 2017, is a big step in the right direction. Governments in the region are taking action to stem and disrupt the flow of drugs, with the support of external partners. But there remains an urgent need to step up our efforts and to ensure a coherent response at the national, regional and international levels.

I would like to briefly lay out some policy recommendations that seek to address these urgent political, social and economic challenges for West Africa, namely:

- Confront openly the political and governance weaknesses, which traffickers exploit

- Strengthen law enforcement for more selective deterrence, focusing on those running the networks rather than their foot soldiers on the ground

- Avoid militarisation of drug policy and related counter-trafficking measures of the kind that some countries have applied at great cost without reducing drug supply

- Regard drug use primarily as a public health problem, not one of criminal justice. Drug users need help, not punishment. We have to put much greater effort and resources into drug treatment facilities and harm-reduction programmes

- Reform drug laws on the basis of existing and emerging minimum health standards and pursue decriminalisation of drug use and low-level, non-violent drug offences. Simple use or possession of any illicit drug by an individual should not be considered a crime and should not be punishable under criminal law

- Intensify cooperation between producing, transit and consuming countries not only on interdiction but also on prevention, treatment and harm reduction.

Today we face a stark choice. We can continue business as usual and see our institutions undermined by drug money and corruption, see increased violence on our streets, see our young exposed to diseases and epidemics and see decades of development efforts compromised. Or we can find the courage to change policies that no longer fit reality. No more sweeping the issue under the carpet and claiming 'it's not our problem'. We need to own the problem and the solutions.

We need to own the

problem and the

solutions

International cooperation

Tackling the impact of drugs through informed, humane and coordinated policy will require a strong and well-coordinated effort. This must be led by African governments, but we need the support of the wider world. Drug trafficking is an international issue – the countries of West Africa should not be left alone to bear the full burden of the struggle against criminal organisations that are often better equipped than the institutions fighting them. The international community must share the burdens created by drug trafficking through West Africa, arriving from South America and Asia and being sold to Europe and North America. Nations whose citizens consume large quantities of illicit drugs must play their part and seek humane ways to reduce demand for those drugs. After all, two-thirds of total revenues of drug trafficking are earned in consuming countries.

For the UN General Assembly Special Session (UNGASS) on drug policy, to be held in April 2016, I would strongly urge countries to not only consider what happens within their borders – where they might have found policies that work at costs that they are willing to bear – but to consider the countries which bear the brunt of the cost in human lives, in loss of human security and in forgone human development. For many of our countries the current system does not work and we need international reform. We hope to be able to count on the solidarity of others, their willingness to listen to what problems we face and thereby to reach an agreement that all can live with. This is what happened at UNGASS 2001 on HIV/AIDS. Africa was the most affected region, but as UN Secretary General Kofi Annan said then:

All of us must recognize AIDS as our problem. All of us must make it our priority. We cannot deal with AIDS by making moral judgements, or refusing to face unpleasant facts – and still less by stigmatizing those who are infected, and making out that it is all their fault.

We must now all recognise the violence related to drug trafficking in some countries and regions, and the lack of access to harm-reduction measures and treatment in others as a problem for all of us

Similarly, we must now all recognise the violence related to drug trafficking in some countries and regions, and the lack of access to harm-reduction measures and treatment in others as a problem for all of us.

Conclusion

Reforming drug laws, offering chronic users proper treatment and not imprisonment, and stopping traffickers from making further inroads in Africa – these are all vital steps. They will take us a long way towards reducing the damaging impact of illegal drugs on communities, families and individuals. They will help to ensure that our young people can grow up healthy and secure. Today we know what works and what does not. It is time to adopt and adapt success stories from across the globe. It is time for a smarter approach to drug policy.

Professor Carl L. Hart

Professor Carl L. Hart is a professor in the Departments of Psychology and Psychiatry at Columbia University. He has published nearly 100 scientific articles in the area of neuropsychopharmacology and is co-author of the textbook *Drugs, Society and Human Behavior* (with Charles Ksir). His book *High Price: A Neuroscientist's Journey of Self-Discovery That Challenges Everything You Know about Drugs and Society* was the 2014 winner of the PEN/E. O. Wilson Literary Science Writing Award. *Fast Company* magazine named Hart one of the Most Creative People for 2014.

Racial Discrimination and the War on Drugs

By Professor Carl L. Hart

Being black is hard work
'Damn, not again' was the exasperated thought

that lingered in my mind as this cold, nondescript, white Canadian customs officer grilled me. 'What brings you to Canada?' she asked in a monotone. Ostensibly, she wanted to know why I was visiting her country, but the fact that my initial answer was insufficient and triggered conspicuous suspicion suggested that she might have been looking for something else, something sinister. Perhaps my gear – athletic wear – in combination with my dreads and melanin-rich skin tone fitted the profile of someone up to no good.

It was a cold November day and I had just landed in the unusually empty Toronto airport, where I was scheduled to catch a connecting flight to Thunder Bay. Yeah, I know. I, too, had never heard of the place prior to being invited to speak in connection with the promotion of my book *High Price* and the documentary film *The House I Live In*. *High Price* had been published just five months earlier, which meant that I had been on the road constantly and was absolutely exhausted. I'm sure my less than bright and puffy eyes were interpreted as belonging to some shady character rather than those of a weary academic in need of a dark, quiet hotel room and a comfortable bed.

This bureaucrat fired a rapid succession of questions, making it clear that she thought I was a drug trafficker. No surprise there. 'Have you been to Canada before?' she continued. 'Are you being paid for your visit?' 'Why are you only staying for two days?' With my best white person voice, I tried to explain my profession – 'I'm a scientist and a professor,' my expertise – 'I study the brain' – and my ties to respectable society, hoping that this would assuage her concerns. She was not impressed. I even did the shameless plug thing, showing her a copy of *High Price* with my face plastered all over the cover. 'Just because you wrote a book,' she replied with an impish smile, 'doesn't mean you're not a drug dealer.' 'Wow,' I softly whispered to myself. And while I was growing increasingly irritated, I maintained a false warm, inviting, outward demeanour. Being black and conscious in the United States has tremendously honed my skills in duplicity. The adroitness of these skills, however, didn't matter because for the next half-hour we checked the inviting organisation's sparse website for any sign of my upcoming talk. There was none. We went through my emails, checking for correspondence between the organisation and myself. Luckily, I found one that suggested I had been invited to give a talk. She carefully read every word, and without emotion, nor any hint that the following line was spoken by a human, she said, 'Have a nice day'. And with that I was allowed to proceed on my way – frustrated, humiliated and with an acute understanding of the phrase 'Being black is hard work.'

I would be lying if I said that this incident initiated my thinking about society's image of the 'typical' drug trafficker or racial discrimination in the enforcement of drug laws. This wasn't the first time I had been 'randomly' selected for questioning by some customs officer, especially outside the US. In an effort to help the reader understand the extent of this and other race-related concerns in the application of

> This wasn't the first time I had been 'randomly' selected for questioning by some customs officer, especially outside the US. In an effort to help the reader understand the extent of this and other race-related concerns in the application of drug policies, this essay addresses the issue of racial discrimination in the War on Drugs

drug policies, this essay addresses the issue of racial discrimination in the War on Drugs. Data and anecdotes come primarily from the US, in large part because there are more available data and the US has strongly encouraged and pressured other nations to adopt policies in line with their own. One caveat to my focus here is that I recognise racial discrimination is not the only form of discrimination that takes place in the enforcement of drug laws. People from lower socio-economic backgrounds regardless of race, individuals who express sexual preferences different from those of the majority, among others, also have been subjected to discrimination in the drug war. A discussion of these other types of discrimination is beyond the scope of the current essay.

Defining racial discrimination and racism

So how did we get to a place where the above indignities have become far too common? The situation is even worse when one considers the egregious examples of black people being killed because they were suspected of selling small amounts of cannabis. Are most white authority figures simply racists? Probably not, but before proceeding I need to clearly define the terms *racial discrimination* and *racist*. So many people have misused and diluted the terms that their perniciousness gets lost when communicating, although the impact on the victims of racial discrimination can continue to fester for a lifetime.

Most English dictionaries define racial discrimination as unjust or prejudicial treatment of different categories of people *on the grounds of race*. Using this definition, intent is necessary before racial discrimination can occur. Put another way, the perpetrator knowingly and deliberately harms a person because the targeted individual is a member of a different race. This nicely describes the behaviour of groups such as the Ku Klux Klan or neo-Nazi skinheads, who are notoriously known for committing abhorrent acts of violence against non-whites and Jewish people.

But this definition seems outdated and inadequate when one considers the fact that black people in the US are about four times more likely to be arrested for cannabis possession than their white counterparts, despite the fact that both groups use cannabis at similar rates. Furthermore, most US lawmakers or police officers do not express an *intent* to have cannabis-related penalties fall disproportionately on the black community. The negative impact of these arrests, however, is no less real regardless of intent. Therefore a more appropriate contemporary definition of racial discrimination might be an action(s) that results in unjust or unfair treatment of persons from a specific racial group. Intent is no longer required. What is required is that the treatment must be unjust or unfair, and that such injustice is disproportionately experienced by at least one racial group. It should also be noted that the terms racial discrimination and racism could be used interchangeably.

So this raises the question about who is a racist. And what about those who unknowingly participate in racial discrimination? The cop who was just doing his job or the well-meaning legislator who proposed the law that resulted in racial discrimination in cannabis arrests: are these individuals racist? Hopefully not. We would need more information, though, before making a definitive determination. For example, if the cop and lawmaker unwittingly participated in racial discrimination but changed their actions when the discrimination was brought to their attention, then it would be inappropriate to label them racists. On the other hand, if these individuals failed to modify their behaviour after being presented with evidence of racial discrimination, then the label racist might be more appropriate.

Institutionalised racism is often much more insidious and difficult to address than the discrimination engaged in by individuals

While racial discrimination is bad enough when exercised by individuals, the most harm is done when discrimination is carried out by institutions such as customs and border protection, the criminal justice system, schools and the media. Institutionalised racism is often much more insidious and difficult to address than the discrimination engaged in by individuals, because there's no specific villain to blame and institutional leaders can easily point to token responses or delay meaningful action indefinitely.

Crack cocaine and racial discrimination

With this as a backdrop, you should know that 25 years ago I began studying neuropsychopharmacology specifically because I wanted to fix the drug addiction problem. I wholeheartedly believed that the poverty and crime in the resource-poor black community from which I came was a direct result of crack cocaine addiction; so I reasoned that if I could cure drug addiction I could fix the poverty and crime in my community. I no longer hold this view, as I have a deeper understanding of what drugs do and don't do. I now recognise that the real problems are misguided policies based on flawed assumptions about drugs and racial discrimination in drug law enforcement.

In the US there has been no drug policy criticised more extensively for its racially discriminatory effects than the Anti-Drug Abuse Acts of 1986 and 1988. These laws set penalties that were 100 times harsher for crack than for powder cocaine violations. Specifically, they required a minimum prison sentence of at least five years for people caught with even small amounts of crack, but not so with powder cocaine.

And since its appearance in the US in late 1984, crack was steeped in a narrative of race and pathology. While powder cocaine came to be regarded as a symbol of luxury and associated with whites, crack was portrayed as producing uniquely addictive, unpredictable and deadly effects and, importantly, was associated with blacks. Perceived problems related to crack were described in terms that were codes for 'blacks'. For example, the drug was seen as being prevalent in 'poor', 'urban' or 'troubled neighbourhoods', 'inner cities' and 'ghettos'. These

These negative associations and anecdotal observations of selective targeting of blacks for prosecution under the federal crack cocaine law prompted growing rumblings concerning media bias and law enforcement unfairness

negative associations and anecdotal observations of selective targeting of blacks for prosecution under the federal crack cocaine law prompted growing rumblings concerning media bias and law enforcement unfairness.

In response, Congress directed the US Sentencing Commission to issue a report examining crack cocaine-related issues. The Commission is the federal agency responsible for, among other tasks, reducing unwarranted sentencing disparities. In February 1995 they issued their report. The report was thorough, examining everything from pharmacology to crime to societal impact. They found that nearly 90 per cent of those sentenced for crack cocaine offences were black, even though the majority of users of the drug were white. They also concluded that crack and powder cocaine are the same drug. It is true that the effects of smoking crack cocaine tend to be more intense than swallowing or snorting powder cocaine, but that increased intensity is due to the route of administration, not the drug itself. Injecting powder cocaine dissolved in water produces nearly identical intense effects as smoking crack cocaine.

The Commission submitted to Congress an amendment to the sentencing guidelines that would have equalised penalties for powder and crack cocaine offences; that is, the crack/powder ratio would have gone from 100:1 to 1:1. Congress passed – and President Bill Clinton signed – legislation disapproving the guideline amendment.

If we go back to our definitions of the terms racial discrimination and racist, it's quite clear that enforcement of the US federal crack cocaine law was being carried out in a racially discriminatory manner. Presumably, this was a horrible, unintended consequence of the policy. But once this information was brought to the attention of the Sentencing Commission, Congress and President Clinton, each had an opportunity to remedy the situation. The Sentencing Commission voted to amend the law, and thereby remove the racial discrimination. As a result, members of the Sentencing Commission were not racist. On the other hand, President Clinton and members of Congress who voted against the amendment were racists, certainly in this case, because they not only failed to take action that would have alleviated the problem, but they also rejected the Sentencing Commission's remedy.

It would take another 15 years and an abundance of vociferous criticism from prominent figures to modify the federal crack cocaine law. In 2007, even presidential candidate Barack Obama added his voice to the chorus of criticism: 'Judges think that's wrong. Republicans think that's wrong. Democrats think that's wrong, and yet it's been approved by Republican and Democratic Presidents because no one has been willing to brave the politics and make it right. That will end when I am President.' On 3 August 2010 President Obama signed the Fair Sentencing Act that reduced – but did not eliminate – the sentencing disparity between crack and powder cocaine from 100:1 to 18:1. This was an important acknowledgement of a bad drug policy, but, to be absolutely clear, any sentencing disparity for crack and powder makes no sense from a scientific or an ethical perspective.

As we think about President Obama's actions within the context of our definitions, it's clear that he too meets the requirement for being

> It would take another 15 years and an abundance of vociferous criticism from prominent figures to modify the federal crack cocaine law

labelled a racist. I recognise that some may find this objectionable because President Obama at least modified the law – he took partial action, whereas his predecessors did not. But it is worth recalling that he clearly recognised the disproportionate negative impact the law was having on blacks. Indeed, he criticised other politicians for failing to exercise courage on this issue. In addition, one of his presidential campaign promises was the elimination of the disparate treatment of the two forms of cocaine under the law. With this in mind, I think Malcolm X posthumously described best President Obama's partial action when he stated, 'If you stick a knife in my back nine inches and pull it out six inches, there is no progress . . . The progress is healing the wound.'

Institutional racism flourishes in the drug war

Malcolm X's words cut even more deeply when one considers the fact that racial discrimination in crack cocaine arrests and prosecutions continues to this day. Blacks still represent more than 80 per cent of those convicted under the federal crack cocaine law. But today, unlike a decade ago, there is virtually no public outrage about this injustice; few prominent public officials are calling for the removal of the differential treatment of crack and powder cocaine.

The inactions of political leaders and others even when they acknowledge the existence of racial discrimination in the enforcement of drug laws reinforces a socio-political environment where certain drugs are deemed evil and any use of these drugs is considered pathological. This, in turn, has provided the fuel for even more inappropriate and draconian policies with an unreasonable goal of eliminating illegal drug use at any cost to marginalised groups. Remarkably, 33 countries, including the US and Indonesia, impose the death penalty for drug trafficking.

Institutional racism flourishes under these conditions and the impact of this situation has been especially devastating for black males. Selective targeting and racial discrimination in the drug war

Selective targeting and racial discrimination in the drug war contribute to some horrifying statistics

contribute to some horrifying statistics. In the US nearly one third of those arrested for drug law violations are black, although drug use rates do not differ by race. Black males comprise about 6 per cent of the general population but make up nearly 40 per cent of the incarcerated population. Moreover, one in three black boys born in the US is projected to spend time in prison. By comparison, only one in 20 white boys faces this damning prospect.

What's worse is that the drug war has, by all evidence, made it acceptable to use deadly force even when the suspect is unarmed as long as there is a *suspicion* of a drug law violation and the suspect is black and male. In February 2012, 18-year-old Ramarley Graham, black, was shot and killed in his Bronx bathroom by a police officer who chased him there in search of cannabis; according to the officer, the teen attempted to flush the drug down the toilet during the confrontation. The officer was initially indicted for manslaughter, but a judge dismissed the charge based on a legal technicality. More recently, in December 2014, 34-year-old Rumain Brisbon of Phoenix, black and unarmed, was shot and killed in his car. He was suspected of selling drugs. The subsequent investigation showed that there was no evidence of drug trafficking. All that was found was a small amount of cannabis and the McDonald's meal he was taking home to his family. The officer who fatally shot Mr Brisbon will not face charges for the shooting either.

In many instances like the ones described above, institutional racism is so pervasive in some organisations (police, customs, etc.) largely because there are few negative consequences for discriminating on the basis of race, even when an innocent person is killed. In some law enforcement and private security organisations, racial profiling remains an important component of training, although this is almost never explicitly acknowledged. Equally important is that racial stereotypes and fears continue to influence the development of drug policy and the enforcement of those policies. It seems as though there's a 'new deadly drug' nearly every year. And when use is associated with a despised group (e.g. blacks), invariably some police officer or politician is interviewed, warning parents about the dangers this drug poses to their children. Usually, after the hysteria has subsided, we discover that the drug in question wasn't as dangerous as we were initially told. In fact, it wasn't even new. But by then the new laws have been passed and they require stiff penalties for possession and distribution of the so-called new, dangerous drug. In fact, the dreadful statistics regarding incarceration rates of black males suggest that this strategy provides an excuse to target black people without explicitly saying so.

There was a time when we were unaware of racial discrimination in the War on Drugs. That time has passed. Discrimination has been extensively documented from profiling black travellers in airports to selectively targeting black neighbourhoods for drug law enforcement. And, sadly, these despicable practices have been exported to other countries, including the UK and Brazil, where blacks are disproportionately stopped and arrested for drug violations. It is long past time for political leaders to be held accountable for their cowardly inactions on drug policy reform that result in racist effects and human rights violations.

> It is long past time for political leaders to be held accountable for their cowardly inactions on drug policy reform that result in racist effects and human rights violations

Nick Clegg

Nick Clegg served as Deputy Prime Minister in Britain's first post-war Coalition Government from 2010 to 2015, and as Leader of the Liberal Democrats from 2007 to 2015. He is the Member of Parliament for Sheffield Hallam, and was previously a Member of the European Parliament.

During his time in office, Clegg was at the heart of decisions surrounding national security and civil liberties, the referenda on electoral reform and Scottish independence, and extensive reforms to the education, health and pensions systems. He was particularly associated with landmark changes to the funding of schools, early years education and the treatment of mental health within the National Health Service.

He remains an outspoken advocate of civil liberties and centre ground politics, of radical measures to boost social mobility and of an internationalist approach to world affairs.

Prospects for Drug Law Reform in the UK

By Nick Clegg

Until fairly recently the UK had been a key player in the international shift away from rigid prohibitionist policies towards a more compassionate and health-focused approach. In the late 1980s Margaret Thatcher's Conservative government responded to alarming levels of injecting drug use by introducing bold harm-reduction reforms that set the tone for drug policy across the whole of Europe. Recognising that the spread of HIV was a greater threat to individual and public health than drug use itself, Thatcher pioneered radical alternatives that sought to manage rather than eliminate the problem: needle exchange, and substituting heroin for prescription methadone.

When the UK's coalition Liberal Democrat/Conservative government was formed in May 2010, there was an unexpected meeting of minds between the two sides on a range of public policy issues, but not, unfortunately, on this one. Beyond some rather technocratic arguments about the use of private finance to fund treatment services, and a focus on abstinence-based programmes, Conservative politicians viewed drug policy reform as a political Pandora's Box – open it a chink and the result would be an uncontrollable whirlwind, alienating the electorate. And to be fair, the same view held true in the opposition Labour party. Neither of the largest parties felt it was in their interests to question the status quo, although in private many senior politicians would say they agreed with the case for reform.

If UK leadership in this area is a shadow of what it was 25 years ago, then what of other European countries? Europe has historically been a major progressive force in the debates at the United Nations and elsewhere, and a test bed for innovative new approaches (for example, the creation of drug consumption rooms in Switzerland, or the ground-breaking decisions by the Portuguese and Czech governments to remove criminal penalties for possession). The unfortunate reality today, however, is that Europe's approach to drug policy is fragmented

Europe's approach to drug policy is fragmented between 28 Member States, none of which has managed to establish a clear leadership position on the international stage

between 28 Member States, none of which has managed to establish a clear leadership position on the international stage. Instead, Europe appears to have ceded leadership to Latin America and the United States.

In government, I did everything I could to use my position as Deputy Prime Minister to speak out publicly about the failure of the War on Drugs, about the unnecessary and inhumane way in which drug users are treated as criminals, and to highlight the positive experience of other countries that took a more compassionate approach. I appointed a colleague as drugs minister (Jeremy Browne, succeeded by Norman Baker), and we used that position to establish the first official UK government review of alternative approaches in other countries. That work concluded that 'there is no apparent correlation between the "toughness" of a country's approach and the prevalence of … drug use'.

This apparently bland finding ought to have been a wake-up call for the political establishment – confirmation that the criminalisation of users does nothing to reduce levels of drug use in society. Instead, most politicians decided to ignore it.

Part of the reason why drug policy reform scares the life out of Westminster is the fiercely negative reaction that has often accompanied attempts at reform. In 2001 the media responded with hysteria to the decision of Commander Brian Paddick to instruct his police officers in Brixton, an area of south London, not to arrest or charge anyone caught in possession of cannabis and focus instead on the dealers. In 2008, after a four-year period during which cannabis was effectively decriminalised following its reclassification from class B to class C, a lurid campaign by the *Daily Mail* (claiming, among other things, that use of the 'killer drug' was the cause of a number of murders) led the then Prime Minister, Gordon Brown, to reverse the decision.

The question is whether the same assumptions about public and press opinion still hold true. Judging from my own experience, I would say the world has moved on. Though I was calling openly for decriminalisation, the reaction was low-key and pragmatic – people were up for the debate. Newspaper editorials were positive. I had supportive letters and emails from members of the public and found that prominent campaigners for drugs reform like Richard Branson and others were keen to work together to make progress.

If anything, the idea that the War on Drugs is winnable has now become entirely threadbare. And the attitude even among those who once led the charge for prohibition is 'Well, that didn't work, so maybe it's time to try something else.' For example, when I suggested in 2014 that drug users shouldn't be sent to prison, the UK's bestselling newspaper, the *Sun*, produced an editorial describing the proposal as 'common sense'.

Public opinion is shifting, too. In 2014 a poll commissioned by the *Sun* found that 65 per cent of people would back a government review of all the reform options, including decriminalisation or legalisation.

The unavoidable conclusion is that public and press opinion has moved on, and the politicians are being left behind. We now have a mismatch between political orthodoxy and political reality, a situation which is by definition unsustainable. The question is therefore not whether reform will happen in the UK, but when, what and how.

> We now have a mismatch between political orthodoxy and political reality, a situation which is by definition unsustainable

The way forward

There are two potential ways forward in my view: the adoption of the Portuguese decriminalisation model, or bespoke cannabis-related reforms.

The first possibility is that we will see a move away from the prosecution and punishment of those who use drugs towards treatment and education – the approach that Portugal has taken since 2001, leading to major criminal justice savings, the freeing up of resources for treatment services and significant falls in problematic drug use and rates of HIV infection.

Similar moves are already happening on the ground in the UK, in part as a response to the pressures which policing budgets are under. In County Durham, the chief constable Mike Barton and the Police and Crime Commissioner (PCC) Ron Hogg have set up the 'Checkpoint' scheme under which a range of low-level non-violent offenders, including some arrested for personal possession, are offered the chance to avoid prosecution if they sign a four-month contract agreeing to take action to tackle the underlying causes of their offending. For the lowest level of drug offences that could involve seeking treatment, attending a drug awareness course, or taking other steps to address underlying problems like homelessness or mental illness. This is a serious and innovative attempt to address the harms associated with drug use rather than hoping (against all the evidence) that punishment alone will deter people from taking drugs.

This is a serious and innovative attempt to address the harms associated with drug use

The experiments in Durham, together with similar moves in Derbyshire, Dorset and Surrey, offer the prospect of *de facto* decriminalisation in parts of the country where police chiefs and their elected Commissioners choose to do so. In Durham, the Checkpoint initiative is subject to rigorous evaluation, and good data demonstrating successful outcomes will make it harder to unpick in the event of a political backlash.

These developments are good news for those concerned with the destructive effects of criminalisation on the lives and careers of the tens of thousands of people who are given a criminal record every year for possession of small amounts of drugs – predominantly cannabis – for their personal use. It will, in turn, help to undo some of the grossly disproportionate impact of drug law policing on black and minority ethnic communities. Research by the campaign group Release has found that black people are six times more likely to be stopped and searched for drugs than white people, despite a lower prevalence of drug use in the black community.

The disadvantage of this grassroots trend, if it continues, is that it will lead to a patchwork of slightly different models in different police force areas. In one sense it could be argued that this is an acceptable outcome, as long as it is sustainable and enjoys local democratic accountability. On the other hand, *de facto* decriminalisation is just that – it enjoys no statutory underpinning, can in theory be unpicked at will, and may be applied inconsistently and unfairly to different individuals. In the longer term, a stable solution will require the amendment of the Misuse of Drugs Act to remove the criminal penalties for possession of small quantities of drugs for personal use, and to insert statutory powers for the police to refer users to appropriate services, or to apply appropriate civil penalties. Ideally, penalties would take the form of administrative fines akin to fixed penalty notices. This is precisely the debate which is currently taking place in Ireland, where politicians are openly advocating the adoption of the Portuguese model and seeing significant police and public support.

> The classification of cannabis became fetishised in the public debate, and the focus quickly turned to whether it was 'safe enough' to downgrade and what 'messages' the move would send to would-be users

Reassessing cannabis

The second area of potential development is specifically around cannabis. Historically, attempts at reform have tended to focus on fighting for the decriminalisation of cannabis as a perceived 'easy win', and shied away from the wider debate around possession of 'harder' drugs like heroin, cocaine and ecstasy. The recent history of cannabis reform is a sorry tale, and campaigners would be wise to think twice about attempting the kind of full frontal assault that saw the drug downgraded from class B to class C in 2004. This relatively innocuous change, which in reality simply gave official sanction to the widespread police practice of turning a blind eye to small-scale cannabis possession, created an easy target for critics. The classification of cannabis became fetishised in the public debate, and the focus quickly turned to whether it was 'safe enough' to downgrade and what 'messages' the move would send to would-be users.

We can remove those harms by substituting civil penalties for criminal sanctions, while continuing to treat cannabis as an illicit substance, and in doing so free up criminal justice and police resources that in turn can be ploughed back into targeting organised crime and public health campaigns

A better approach to cannabis would be to start from the truthful assumption that it can be harmful to physical and mental health, although not at the more serious end of the scale of harm (alcohol and tobacco, for example, can be much more harmful). The question then becomes whether the legal framework governing its use and availability is the best framework for reducing those harms.

One thing we can say with confidence, thanks to the work conducted by the Home Office, is that the criminalisation of cannabis users does nothing to reduce cannabis use in society: those countries that have decriminalised use haven't seen a big spike in prevalence. It logically follows that the application of criminal penalties to cannabis users constitutes harm inflicted on individuals for no effective social purpose. We can remove those harms by substituting civil penalties for criminal sanctions, while continuing to treat cannabis as an illicit substance, and in doing so free up criminal justice and police resources that in turn can be ploughed back into targeting organised crime and public health campaigns.

Of course, these arguments apply equally to the users of other drugs, too, but it may be more politically palatable to start with cannabis and to demonstrate that a robust system can be designed that is more effective at reducing the health harms of the drug than the existing system of prohibition. The key to unlocking the politics of this is to design a system of civil penalties that can command public confidence, rather than simply saying the police should 'look away' when they see the drug being used. This is where schemes like Checkpoint come in, by demonstrating effective new ways of changing behaviour which don't resort to the criminal law.

A more achievable short-term goal may be to secure a change in the law around medical cannabis. The medical benefits of cannabis are well established for certain conditions that often do not respond well to more conventional treatments. In the UK one cannabis product, Sativex (essentially a concentrated cannabis oil), is available on prescription, but it is expensive, only available in a few areas, and can only be provided for the treatment of spasticity associated with multiple sclerosis. A change in the law to allow doctors to prescribe medical-grade herbal cannabis would bring relief to hundreds of patients up and down the country suffering from pain, loss of appetite and other symptoms – many of whom are currently risking prosecution. This isn't a radical change and would bring us into line with other countries like Germany, Italy, Canada, the US and Israel. More importantly, it is a question of basic humanity. An effective campaign in this area could win political backers from all parties.

Prospects for the UK

What are the longer-term prospects for the UK? One key question, as we witness the US – the country that invented the War on Drugs – steadily moving away from domestic prohibition of cannabis, is whether full legalisation of cannabis is ever likely to be a realistic goal here. At the moment the political barriers appear insurmountable. The good news is that with increasing numbers of US states establishing formal regulated schemes for recreational use, we are rapidly moving from a world in which legalisation could be legitimately described as a 'leap in the dark' to a world where we have empirical data showing the advantages and disadvantages of the move. The emerging evidence is broadly positive – no dramatic increase in use, lower levels of crime, no spike in road traffic accidents and substantial tax revenues. If that continues to be the case, other jurisdictions will follow suit – including perhaps Canada where the new government was elected with a specific manifesto commitment to legally regulate cannabis. Then the momentum for change on this side of the Atlantic will only grow, and may begin to snowball much more quickly than people expect, so that in 10 years' time it is not unreasonable to envisage a legal market here in the UK.

The momentum for change on this side of the Atlantic will only grow, and may begin to snowball much more quickly than people expect

Political parties that grasp what is happening internationally and start to articulate the positive arguments for change will, in my view, reap significant rewards. While the politics of drug law reform in the UK are currently stuck in a rut, we can take comfort from the trends and indicators discussed here. Well-organised campaigns are likely to see significant breakthroughs in the years to come, and I hope that in the long term the UK can once again take its place as an international leader when it comes to enlightened drug policy.

Pavel Bém

Pavel Bém is a Czech physician and politician, who was a Member of Parliament and served two terms as Mayor of the City of Prague. He is also a member of the Global Commission on Drug Policy.

Bém studied medicine at Charles University in Prague, specialising in psychiatry and subsequently devoting most of his career in medicine to drug abuse prevention and treatment.

Progressive Drug Policy in the Czech Republic Since the Velvet Revolution: Public Health or Public Safety? Both ...

● ● ● ● ● ● ●

By Pavel Bém

The Czech Republic (formerly part of Czechoslovakia) has inherited many archetypal stigmas and other harmful practices from its Communist past. These include a moral distortion of values and norms due to the lack of freedom and entrenched human rights violations; a perverse judicial system persecuting innocent people; and a socialist paradigm based on the assumption that everybody should share the same level of poverty.

On the other hand, as far as illicit drug policies are concerned, we have also inherited quite a well-developed health-care system, accessible to most stigmatised and socially excluded groups, including injecting drug users.

In 1989 Czechoslovakia's Communist leadership somewhat reluctantly admitted that the country was 'infected' by illicit drugs imported from the 'West'. Rough estimates showed approximately 10,000 injecting drug users. However, these were injecting mainly domestically manufactured drugs like 'brown' (hydrocodone) and 'pervitin' (methamphetamine).

> In 1989, Czechoslovakia's Communist leadership somewhat reluctantly admitted that the country was 'infected' by illicit drugs imported from the 'West'

After the fall of the Iron Curtain later that year and the subsequent dissolution of the Warsaw Pact, Czechoslovakia, and later the Czech Republic, opened its borders and became a player in all European and international markets, including the manufacture, trafficking and distribution of illicit drugs.

Illicit drug supplies increased dramatically, as did the number of small-scale dealers and the activities of organised crime in general. Consequently, the number of problem drug users (PDUs) also rose significantly.

Yet the public health impact of this sharp increase in illicit drug use was not dramatic, due to a combination of the Communist regime's pilot harm-reduction services and the in-depth, pragmatic drug policy changes in the transitional period after 1989.

Adoption and implementation of new policies in the nineties

During the early 1990s these newly adopted drug policies, and their implementation at national and local levels, sought to bring the emerging illicit drugs phenomenon under control. For example, syringe and needle exchange programmes and opioid substitution treatment services were introduced in almost all cities and regions at risk.

> Czech drug policy proved to be an effective set of tools and instruments, promoting public health and guaranteeing public safety

And it worked. Czech drug policy proved to be an effective set of tools and instruments, promoting public health and guaranteeing public safety. HIV prevalence among injecting drug users is one of the lowest worldwide, as are mortality and overall morbidity. Furthermore, drug-related crimes do not generate the unbearable social and economic costs they do in many other European and non-European countries.

There are many interlinked reasons why Czech drug policy has produced such favourable long-term outcomes.

Having a clear, consistent strategy with sustainable funding was vital. Early adoption of the National Drug Strategy (1993), and a well-balanced white paper outlining drug supply and drug demand reduction measures, created the administrative infrastructure needed for drug policy implementation at both national and local level. This was critical to ensuring sustainability and continuity amid the frequent political changes that are typical in young democracies. Also, adopting a sustainable financial model for supporting the non-governmental sector was crucial for the delivery of successful harm-reduction services.

Adopting a sustainable financial model for supporting the non-governmental sector was crucial for the delivery of successful harm-reduction services

The Czech approach did not stop at the national level. Public health policies were implemented at the local level – harm-reduction services, like needle exchange schemes for injecting drug users; comprehensive treatment plans including methadone and buprenorphine maintenance programmes for severe opioid addicts; and outreach programmes accessing hidden populations of PDUs. As a result, approximately 70 per cent of Czech PDUs are currently in contact with treatment services, compared to 20 per cent in 1993. In the area of drug laws, decriminalising the possession of illicit drugs for personal use and drug use itself (driven primarily by human rights considerations) was a key factor in delivering success during the 1990s. Similarly, alternatives to incarceration for users involved in petty property crimes and other non-violent offences were introduced. This was coupled with a call for law enforcement to focus on higher levels of organised drug crime, rather than on drug users.

Education and training played a key role, as well. For example, designing and implementing specialised undergraduate and postgraduate training programmes for addiction specialists, at Charles University, significantly upgraded the quality of multidisciplinary teams within the treatment services network.

Finally, the government adopted Minimum Standards of Care (MSC) for drug users that introduced quality assurance measures within the treatment network, established the National Drug Monitoring Centre, and developed relevant Minimum Evaluation Standards. All these measures guaranteed that public resources were being invested effectively. (The MSC also defined provisions for delivery of harm-reduction services, like needle exchange schemes, outreach services, accessibility of low-threshold treatment centres, substitution programmes, etc.).

> ## In combination, these policies and measures have been responsible for one of the lowest rates of drug-induced deaths in the EU (3.9 cases per million)

In combination, these policies and measures have been responsible for one of the lowest rates of drug-induced deaths in the EU (3.9 cases per million) . Likewise, HIV and HCV prevalence among injecting drug users is low. The prevalence of opioid and amphetamine problem drug use has stabilised, while the prevalence of cannabis use, although still high, is decreasing.

Changing attitudes, practices and approaches

Police and special drug squad practices, prosecutors' attitudes and court decisions are key to the cost-effectiveness and sustainability of drug policies, as are the legal frameworks covering these policies. On the law enforcement side, decriminalisation had the desired effect of reducing drug-related arrests, while releasing resources and removing a barrier for problematic users to seek help.

The percentage of drug arrests in the Czech Republic is favourably low: out of 130,000 arrestable offences a year, less than 2 per cent are for drug-related crimes. The rate of arrest specifically for drug use, and possession for personal use, in the Czech Republic was the lowest among all EU countries.

> Decriminalisation had the desired effect of reducing drug-related arrests, while releasing resources and removing a barrier for problematic users to seek help

Unfortunately, the Czech Republic has not been immune to the irrational and populist War on Drugs rhetoric that emerged worldwide in the 1990s and led to dramatic repressive shifts in policy, disproportionately penalising drug possession for personal use in many countries.

As a result, a new Czech penal code was adopted in 1998, criminalising the possession of illicit drugs for personal use. The proponents of criminalisation expected reductions in the availability of illicit drugs, as well as decreases in both prevalence and incidence of illicit drug use. They also assumed that neither negative health indicators related to drug use nor the social costs of drug abuse would increase.

This was a critical moment, with most Czech experts, NGOs and significant parts of the press fearing the new legislation was a case of wishful thinking that would have dramatic, unintended negative consequences, similar to those seen elsewhere in the world.

Immediately after the parliamentary vote (defying President Havel´s veto), the Czech government decided to launch a scientific evaluation of the new drug law – something few if any governments globally have ever done. The ultimate goal was to measure the expected benefits and to explore potential unintended negative impacts.

Impact Analysis Project: a careful evaluation

The Impact Analysis Project (PAD), which produced a series of studies, including a cost-benefit analysis, was a complex exercise, combining qualitative and quantitative research methods, measuring direct as well as indirect costs of drug use.

The results of two years of scientific assessment and evaluation were both unique and interesting: all the hypotheses predicting positive effects from criminalisation were rejected. The evaluation also showed there was no deterrent effect from the new drug legislation on problem drug users who suffer most of the harms stemming from illicit drug use.

There were also indications of increasing availability of illicit drugs. All illicit drugs were judged to be more available to those with zero experience, and hard drugs were judged to be more available to those with experience of drug use. Long-term price stability on the criminal market also indicated that the new punitive law had no impact on the availability of illicit drugs. Both cannabis and ecstasy use increased in the studied period, and use of heroin and pervitine – two of the major so-called 'hard drugs' – remained stable. The number of new cases of drug use in the general population increased. For example, there was a significant increase in illicit drug use among 16-year-olds, particularly cannabis, from 1997 to 2001, with a similar trend in the general population.

Over the two-year period assessed, the criminalisation of possession of drugs for personal use was also judged to be economically disadvantageous. It caused a waste of resources of at least CZK161,260 (€5,821) per case detected by the police.

Conclusions

The 1998 drug law caused severe negative consequences and additional social, public health and economic costs, while having no positive impacts. After 2001, broader expert and public debate around the new law, based on clear scientific evidence, and with the support of the Czech media, prevented further negative changes in Czech drug policy or criminal justice practices. Consequently, the overall burden and cost of this punitive 'legal experiment' was minimised.

The PAD project could be considered an effective 'harm-reduction' intervention at the drug policy level. It provided politicians, decision-makers and the media with scientific evidence to expose wrong political decisions and immediately correct their misplaced expectations. Most importantly, it also facilitated the reintroduction of decriminalisation in 2010. It provided hard evidence that without our progressive policies we would not be seeing the beneficial outcomes around mortality, blood-borne diseases, criminal justice and effective use of resources that we do today.

Looking at the global picture, the Czech experience of scientifically assessing the impacts of criminalising drug use, then reversing the decision and decriminalising use, is an all-too-rare example of evidence-led drug policy making.

> The Czech experience of scientifically assessing the impacts of criminalising drug use, then reversing the decision and decriminalising use, is an all-too-rare example of evidence-led drug policy making

The following conclusions can be drawn from the Czech experience:

1. The War on Drugs is a lost war. Drugs are harmful – but repression is even more so.

2. Public health and public safety should come first. They are not mutually exclusive. Availability of services and wide introduction of harm-reduction interventions to PDUs is a key factor in policy effectiveness.

3. Drug users are not criminals, and the incarceration of drug users generates more harm than positive effects.

4. Drug markets should be regulated instead of prohibited. Prohibition generates huge unintended negative consequences and thus increases the ultimate social and economic cost of drug use. Different drugs need different degrees of regulation.

5. Drug trafficking fuels violence and corruption and is directly linked to unregulated markets. Scientific evidence must be continuously brought to the public audience in order to prevent wishful thinking, especially among politicians and decision-makers.

6. Education, prevention and treatment can reduce the overall harm of drug use to society.

7. One size does not fit all. It is time to rethink and explore alternatives – with new drug policies based on evidence, not rhetoric.

Peter Dunne

Peter Dunne was born in Christchurch, New Zealand, and graduated from the University of Canterbury with a Master of Arts degree with Honours in Political Science. He also studied business administration at Massey University.

Dunne has been a Member of Parliament since 1984, holding the north-west Wellington seats of Ohariu, Onslow Ohariu-Belmont and Ohariu.

Since 1995, he has held a variety of ministerial roles and is currently New Zealand's Minister of Internal Affairs, Associate Minister of Health and Associate Minister of Conservation.

Regulating the New Psychoactives Market: The New Zealand Experiment

By Peter Dunne

Background

New Zealand, like many countries globally, has struggled to deal with the rapid development and availability of new psychoactive substances.

Being a small, geographically isolated country presents both advantages and challenges when addressing such an issue. As many other nations sought to apply blanket ban solutions to the issue, New Zealand chose to take an innovative, harm-minimisation approach through regulating the market. This essay looks back at the approach taken and the lessons to be learned from it.

> New Zealand chose to take an innovative, harm-minimisation approach through regulating the market

New Zealand's first significant encounters with synthetic psychoactive substances, often referred to as 'legal highs', can be traced back to the late 1990s and early 2000s when benzylpiperazine (BZP) use grew significantly, due to a lack of any regulation of the compound.

This lack of regulation was in large part due to New Zealand's overarching drug law – the Misuse of Drugs Act 1975 (MoDA) – not recognising newly developed drugs. The MoDA had been developed in a time when cannabis, heroin, LSD and cocaine by and large dominated the illicit drug market.

Although manufacture and sale of BZP was eventually banned in 2008 through an amendment to the MoDA, the issue of New Zealand's ageing legislation failing to keep pace with rapid technological advances, an increasingly globalised marketplace and an unabated demand for psychoactive substances led to an untenable situation as new psychoactive substances (NPS) proliferated.

The lack of regulation of NPS meant that, for a considerable period during the early 2000s, sale and supply of them largely flew under the radar. Products with titles such as Kronic, Kryptonite and Apocalypse were being retailed in a variety of small outlets such as corner shops, video stores, adult shops and alternative lifestyle/head shops. The products were often displayed on the counter alongside confectionery and everyday household products and little thought was given to them by the majority of customers.

Unsurprisingly, awareness of the availability and their associated harm grew as their popularity increased. As NPS proliferated, stories of users' serious adverse effects and issues with addiction became increasingly common. The lack of any age restriction other than for smokeable products, for which purchase was restricted to those 18 and over under New Zealand's Smokefree Environments Act 1990, meant that young people were particularly adversely impacted by their availability.

In the wake of the rapidly evolving NPS market, in 2007 the government asked the New Zealand Law Commission, an independent statutory advisory body, to review New Zealand's drug law, the result of which was a comprehensive 340-page report in April 2011 which proposed 'a new regime with its own criteria and approval process for regulating new substances'.

Recognising the burgeoning use and associated adverse effects of NPS, in April 2010, as Associate Minister of Health with responsibility for alcohol, drugs and addiction, among other things, I moved to address the legislative void, introducing the Misuse of Drugs Amendment Bill 2010, to provide for the introduction of measures known as Temporary Drug Class Notices (TCDNs).

These TCDNs empowered the Minister of Health to specify as a temporary class drug 'a substance, preparation, mixture, or article that is not a Class A, Class B, or Class C controlled drug, a restricted substance, or a precursor substance, but that the Minister "is satisfied poses, or may pose, a risk of harm to individuals or to society"'.

The ban would last 12 months, with the potential for a further 12-month extension if necessary. The breathing space provided by the ban period allowed for two separate streams of work to be undertaken: firstly, evidence would become available demonstrating that the substance in question was either dangerous enough to justify scheduling under the MoDA itself (a time-consuming, evidence-based process), or of a low enough risk that no further action was required when the ban lapsed; and, secondly, and perhaps more importantly from a longer-term perspective, it gave the government time to work on a detailed response to the Law Commission's review of the MoDA.

Temporary Class Drug Notices appeared to be successful initially, with all 43 synthetic cannabis products being retailed at the time immediately banned under TCDN following enactment in early August 2011. As I said in a media release at the time:

> Any new products will be dealt with as they arrive. From the date a temporary class drug order comes into force on a substance, the import, export, manufacture, supply and sale of the drug concerned will become illegal. The notices will be able to be applied to particular synthetic cannabis products, or particular substances that may be in any given product. These products change frequently, and new ones are put on the market with a different ingredient or two. We will basically be able to capture them all.

In hindsight, TCDNs were a bit like applying one band-aid at a time while walking through a field of thistles. Each time a TCDN was issued for a substance – and it should be noted that they were for identified substances, rather than products – that substance was 'tweaked' and re-entered the market.

Over time, as the industry adjusted to TCDNs, their new formulations were developed, packaged and ready to be retailed immediately when an existing substance was identified and banned. The regime may in fact have had the perverse effect of bringing newer, more harmful substances to the market as replacements for those that were banned. An added

As the industry adjusted to TCDNs, their new formulations were developed, packaged and ready to be retailed immediately when an existing substance was identified and banned

complication was that, because only identified substances were banned, the brand names continued to be used, leading to confusion about whether banned substances were still being sold or not.

The extent to which the industry was able to work around the new law was not immediately apparent, however, and for an extended period there was widespread support for my 'you put 'em up, I'll knock 'em down' challenge to the NPS industry. It is fair to say they accepted that challenge with alacrity.

The Psychoactive Substances Act

As the initial TCDN extended into its second 12-month period, it was clear that a new regime was needed, as had been recommended by the Law Commission. Although the MoDA needed work to bring it into the twenty-first century, priority was given to finding a lasting solution to the NPS situation.

In a significant shift for New Zealand's drug policy, the government agreed to a system to regulate, rather than apply a blanket ban to, NPS. There were, in my view, two overriding reasons for this:

1. New Zealand's constitutional conventions did not support making illegal items or activities that may in fact be harmless or low risk through broad-brush/indiscriminate regulation.

2. Prohibition had been seen to be a failure on a number of levels across a variety of circumstances, and the NPS situation in particular, given its fluidity and global nature, did not lend itself to an outright ban.

The culmination of a significant amount of work by my office and the Ministry of Health was the Psychoactive Substances Bill, which I introduced to the New Zealand Parliament on 26 February 2013. The bill – the Psychoactive Substances Act 2013 – became law in July that year, following lengthy delays within the government's legislative timetable. Parliamentary support for the bill was almost unanimous, passing by 119 to 1, with the single vote against arising from concerns around the potential for animal testing.

The Act, as I stated in its introductory speech, was to end the dangerous game of cat and mouse by banning the import, the manufacture, the sale, the supply and the possession of psychoactive substances. The Act's key element, in my view, was the reversal of the onus of proof by making all psychoactive substances illegal, unless the industry could prove their products were low-risk.

> The Act, as I stated in its introductory speech, was to end the dangerous game of cat and mouse by banning the import, the manufacture, the sale, the supply and the possession of psychoactive substances

The burden of proof had been an expensive millstone around the neck of New Zealand's government agencies as they were required to undertake a significant amount of product testing to determine what substances were involved before any move could be made to ban them. Even when testing was undertaken, in some cases the compounds were so novel as to be effectively unidentifiable, with a lack of reference standards available.

The Act also created a Psychoactive Substances Regulatory Authority and an expert advisory committee. The Authority was responsible for granting licences for the import and manufacture of psychoactive substances, and, on the advice of the expert committee, for approving psychoactive products for sale if they had been shown to pose no more than a low risk of harm to the user.

The response

Public feedback on the new legislation was mixed. Advocates of measured and proportionate drug policy applauded the Act, recognising the departure from previous approaches that it represented, and in some cases hoping that it might lead to changes in other areas of drug policy. There were many, however, who wanted an outright ban and were prepared to settle for nothing less, despite the impracticalities of such an approach.

Local government was particularly outspoken, despite being given the power to determine where in their districts retail outlets could be located. The majority of jurisdictions argued for an outright ban, and claimed that, by allowing them to determine where products might be sold, the government was essentially offloading its problems on to others to solve. This view was disappointing, but sadly reflective of a local government sector that likes to cherry-pick which aspects of regulation it is responsible for and which it would prefer not to have to deal with.

There were two significant inclusions in the legislation which would prove controversial for months following its enactment, ultimately ending in an amendment to the Act.

First, the Act allowed an interim period whereby products that were currently being sold were permitted

The majority of jurisdictions argued for an outright ban, and claimed that, by allowing them to determine where products might be sold, the government was essentially offloading its problems on to others to solve

to continue being sold while the full testing regime and regulations were being developed.

The Act prohibited the sale of NPS from almost all retail outlets with the exception of adult stores and dedicated R18 retailers which, although reducing the number of outlets from an estimated 4,000+ to around 150, had the unintended effect of increasing their visibility, with queues forming on occasion due to the vastly reduced accessibility of products. Internet sale was also permitted.

There were ongoing claims that products that continued to be sold during the interim period were causing harm, though anecdotally it was suggested by some in the medical profession that some presenting to emergency departments were blaming NPS to cover the use of other, more harmful, illicit substances. Given the relative novelty of the testing regime there was little chance to disprove such claims.

The second was the issue of animal testing, which, while not specified in legislation, was required for products to be shown to be low-risk. The Ministry of Health advised that for the testing regime to be robust it must include animal testing to ensure products were of low risk before they were trialled in human test subjects, similar to the testing required for pharmaceutical products. This created significant unrest among the public, which was uncomfortable with the notion of animals suffering so that people could take recreational drugs.

These two issues, coupled with daily sensationalist media coverage of queues outside stores, stories of allegedly severe adverse reactions to NPS products and protest

> Daily sensationalist media coverage of queues outside stores, stories of allegedly severe adverse reactions to NPS products and protest marches across the country by animal rights groups, were to lead to an urgent revision of the Act

179

marches across the country by animal rights groups, were to lead to
an urgent revision of the Act, which passed unopposed, albeit with
14 abstentions by New Zealand's Green Party.

The interim period for existing products was discarded, making way
for a clean-slate approach with all products having to be proven to be
low-risk before they could return to, or newly enter, the market.

New clauses were added to the primary legislation banning any use
of data derived from animal tests with the exception of that used to
show a product posed more than a low risk of harm.

In one fell swoop these changes took all products from the shelves
and pushed back by years any likelihood of them returning. It is in this
hiatus that we continue to find ourselves today.

Looking back

Hindsight is, as they say, a wonderful thing, and this case is no
exception. Although much of the adverse coverage of the regime
was hyperbolic, sensationalist and in many cases hugely ill-informed,
allowing sales to continue during the interim period was a mistake.
There was simply too much baggage from the previous decade of an
unregulated NPS market to allow an unbiased, rational discussion of
the approach to succeed.

That said, the interim period had been explicitly included to prevent
a black market filling the void, and the government retained the power
to remove any existing products should they prove to be problematic.
That opportunity was lost and there are semi-regular reports now
of black market operations in NPS, although availability is, I believe,
hugely reduced and reported adverse effects have also diminished to
an almost imperceptible level.

The Psychoactive Substances Regulatory Authority, established
and tasked with implementing the regulatory regime, was in my view
under-resourced for the complexity and size of the task it faced. The NPS
industry was awash with cash and its legal counsels were highly active
in pushing their clients' interests. The Authority's approach of treating

NPS like any other regulated product was naïve and it failed to gauge the public antipathy to the products and its desire for a firmer approach.

The animal testing issue was part of a wider movement globally away from a reliance on animals to newer computer modelling and in-vitro testing processes. This issue already had an extensive history in the cosmetics industry, which has seen animal testing for cosmetics banned across the EU and in a number of other jurisdictions.

Looking back, it should have been foreseen that opposition to animal testing of NPS would become a feature of this process. The ban on using data from animal tests, while setting back the process of bringing low-risk NPS to market I would estimate by a conservative 5–10 years, will I hope add momentum to the alternative testing movement and encourage further progress in the development of alternative testing regimes.

Now and the future

The amended Act saw NPS products removed from shelves overnight, and the issue, which had rumbled on for so long, died down almost as quickly. In the space of around 24 hours media interest dwindled to almost nothing. The zombie hordes that had been predicted to descend on hospitals and alcohol and drug treatment centres suffering extreme withdrawal never materialised. To a degree this was because many had seen the writing on the wall and stockpiled products, but it also underlined the fact that the media coverage had outrageously overhyped the issue.

Effectively, NPS and their regulation have been pushed under the carpet until such time as a manufacturer submits a product to the Authority here for approval as low-risk.

Despite the somewhat panicked amendment to the legislation, it remains intact and ready to deal with whatever may be thrown at it in the future, be it newly synthesised substances and products, or long-ago discovered compounds lurking or stashed in the basements of pharmaceutical companies around the world.

Sooner or later new testing regimes will be developed and approved and the regulated market will be tested – as has been seen the world over, the NPS issue shows no signs of diminishing and it is my opinion that the complexity of the issue will not abate, but continue to increase.

The Psychoactive Substances Act future-proofs New Zealand drug policy with respect to NPS, and may provide a sound model in years to come for assessing other illicit drugs.

The Act is a response for New Zealand, to New Zealand's situation, both cultural and geographical. It is not a one-size-fits-all for all drugs and all nations. But it is a model which I believe has great merit and I hope is actively considered by others as they seek to address what often seems like an intractable and vexing issue.

> The Act is a response for New Zealand, to New Zealand's situation, both cultural and geographical. It is not a one-size-fits-all for all drugs and all nations

Epilogue: From Awareness to Action

· · · · · · · · ·

By Sam Branson

Its been nearly five decades since US President Richard Nixon declared drugs 'public enemy number one', and the global War on Drugs that has been raging ever since has delivered far more than just angry rhetoric. It has produced immense suffering on a catastrophic scale.

Over one trillion dollars has been wasted; millions of people have been incarcerated and hundreds of thousands killed in the violence that this war has created. It has truly spun out of control.

The illegal drug market is a global trade controlled entirely by criminals, turning over $350 billion every year to fuel illegal activities. These illegal activities eat away at the very fabric of our societies and crush the potential for a harmonious existence on this planet.

Ending the series of failures discussed in this book is not simply a matter of changing global or national policy. It's a matter of winning the hearts and minds of people everywhere. We need to defy misinformation and stereotypes and counter the current hysteria with fact-based evidence.

When speaking about the war on drugs, I often encounter the same reactions as those seen when discussing the climate debate. Basic instincts trump scientific evidence, and fear and stereotypes stand in the way of rational considerations about alternative approaches to the problem.

And yet, change is happening. Over the last few years several US States did the 'unthinkable': they legalised and regulated the sale of cannabis. Uruguay too has already done it and Canada is on its way to doing the same. As I write these lines, Ireland is considering the decriminalisation of all drug possession for personal use. All of this is a huge step forward for an issue that affects each and every one of us all around the world.

But none of these changes can happen overnight. In most cases they begin as conversations between ordinary people impacted in countless ways by decades of prohibition. From people who use drugs, to those who have lost a loved one to overdose or disease, from law enforcement officers frustrated with the undiminished power of organised crime, to taxpayers concerned about the price tag of needless criminalisation and mass incarceration – there is now an ever-growing movement of people on the front lines and on the fringes who are no longer willing to put up with the status quo.

My own journey began in 2011 when I decided to do my own part to educate people about the staggering facts surrounding this issue. I made a film with my production company, Sundog Pictures, called *Breaking the Taboo*. The intentions of this film were to unpack the complexity of the drug debate for people in a way that painted a truly global picture. It became a critically acclaimed documentary that shines a spotlight on just how devastating the impact of the War on Drugs has been, along the entire value chain of the global drug trade, from producers to consumers. Ever since *Breaking the Taboo* premiered in December 2012, it has been highly effective in opening the drug debate to a broader audience by presenting a compelling and irrefutable case for change.

For all social movements, the real challenge is to move from awareness to engagement and to understand what role we can each play in bringing about tangible, lasting change. If governments are to end the War on Drugs, people like you and me will have to push them there, bringing others on board along the way. What it takes is the difference between 'slacktivism' and activism, between hitting the 'like' button on a social media page and actually making a lasting contribution.

Thankfully, there are many different entry points for civil engagement, from global campaigns to grassroots efforts. Below are some of the initiatives you might consider joining or supporting to further the cause. They are helping advance the debate and encourage governments to do the right thing:

Stop the Harm

Stop the Harm is a diverse, broad, and powerful movement of NGOs from around the world who have united around one common purpose: rectifying the catastrophic failures of the current global drug policy regime through campaigning for a new course firmly grounded in health, compassion and human rights.

www.stoptheharm.org

Support. Don't punish.

Support. Don't Punish. is a global advocacy campaign calling for better drug policies that prioritise public health and human rights. The campaign aims to promote drug policy reform, and to change laws and policies that impede access to harm reduction interventions.

www.supportdontpunish.org

Count the Costs

The War on Drugs creates massive costs, resulting from an enforcement-led approach that puts organised crime in control of the trade.

It is time to **count these costs** and explore the alternatives, using the best available evidence, to deliver a safer, healthier and more just world.

www.countthecosts.org

Anyone's Child

Anyone's Child: Families for Safer Drug Control is a network of families whose lives have been wrecked by the UK's drug laws and are now campaigning to change them. www.anyoneschild.org

It is often said that there are significant generational gaps in attitudes towards illicit drugs and drug use. That may be true, but every day that we wait for the next generation to act and tackle the injustice and insanity that is the global War on Drugs, lives will be lost, money will be wasted and opportunities will be missed. There has never been a better opportunity to break the taboo. Educate yourself and find your own way of having an impact. It will help to pave the way for a more harmonious and sustainable existence for us all in the years to come.

www.anyoneschild.org

Glossary

Alternative development

Drug crops are mainly grown in areas where isolation and poverty are inherent, and farmers are unable to obtain sufficient income from legal activities due to lack of markets, conflict, marginal land and absence of basic infrastructure. Alternative development aims to provide sustainable legal livelihoods to communities that cultivate illicit drug crops, for example through crop substitution programmes.

CND – United Nations Commission on Narcotic Drugs

With representatives of 53 Member States, the CND is the body that considers all matters pertaining to the aims and implementation of the UN Drug Conventions, approves most of the UN drug-control budget, and is the governing body of the UN Office on Drugs and Crime.

Decriminalisation

Most commonly used to describe the removal or non-enforcement of criminal penalties for use or possession of small quantities of drugs or paraphernalia for personal use (sometimes also used in reference to other minor drug offences). While no longer criminal, possession still remains an offence subject to administrative or civil sanctions, such as fines or referrals to services.

Global Commission on Drug Policy

A group of former and current world leaders, businesspeople and experts bringing to the international level an informed, science-based discussion about humane and effective ways to reduce the harm caused by drugs to people and societies.

Harm reduction

'Harm reduction' refers to policies, programmes and practices that aim to reduce the negative health, social and economic consequences of using legal and illegal psychoactive drugs for people unable or unwilling to stop. The defining feature is a focus on the prevention of harm, rather than on prevention of drug use itself. Approaches typically described as 'harm-reduction measures' include opioid substitution programmes, syringe exchanges or medically supervised injection facilities.

IDU
Injecting drug user

Legalisation
The process of ending prohibitions on the production, distribution and use of a drug for other than medical or scientific uses. In the drug policy context 'legalisation' is generally used to refer to a policy position advocating 'legal regulation' or 'legally regulated drug markets' for currently prohibited drugs.

NPS – Novel/New Psychoactive Substances
Generally (although not exclusively) this term is used to describe recently emerging synthetically produced drugs used for non-medical or scientific purposes that are not subject to control under the United Nations Single Convention on Narcotic Drugs 1961 and the United Nations Convention on Psychotropic Drugs 1971 (although some nation states may act unilaterally and regulate or prohibit certain NPS under domestic legislation).

NSP – Needle-syringe exchange/provision programmes
A type of harm-reduction initiative that provides clean needles and syringes to people who inject drugs to reduce the risk of health harms, including transmission of HIV and hepatitis C.

OST – Opioid substitution therapy
OST supplies illicit drug users with a long-lasting replacement drug, such as methadone or buprenorphine, which is usually administered orally in a supervised clinical setting. In many developed countries it is a fundamental component of the response to the dual public health problems of injecting drug use and HIV and other blood-borne disease transmission.

Prevalence
A measure of how many drug users there are in a country or community and how they are distributed across the population.

Prohibition
The establishment of criminal sanctions for the production, distribution and possession of certain drugs (for other than medical or scientific uses). This term is used in reference to the international drug control regime as defined by the UN conventions and treaties of 1961, 1971 and 1988, as well as domestic legislation (sanctions varying widely).

Regulation

The set of legally enforceable rules that govern the market for a drug, involving application of different controls depending on drug risks and needs of local environments. Includes regulation of production (licensed producers), products (price, potency, packaging), availability (licensed vendors, location of outlets, age controls) and marketing (advertising and branding). Examples include the regulated recreational cannabis markets in the US states of Colorado, Oregon, Washington and Alaska.

SIF – Supervised injecting/injection facilities

SIFs are also known as 'drug consumption rooms', 'injecting rooms', 'safe injecting facilities' or sometimes pejoratively in the populist media as 'shooting galleries'. They are places where people can inject illicit drugs, supervised by nurses and social workers. The first opened in Switzerland, in the 1980s. There are now approximately 90 SIFs worldwide – the majority of these in European countries.

UNGASS on Drugs

The United Nations General Assembly Special Session, or UNGASS, is a meeting of all UN Member States to assess and debate global issues such as health, gender, or, in this case, international drug policy. The next session will be held in New York in April 2016.

UNODC – United Nations Office on Drugs and Crime

UNODC is a UN body aimed at developing a coordinated, comprehensive response to illicit trafficking in and abuse of drugs, crime prevention and criminal justice, international terrorism and political corruption. These goals are pursued through research, guidance and support to governments in the adoption and implementation of various crime, drug, terrorism and corruption-related conventions, treaties and protocols, as well as technical/financial assistance.

Further reading and sources for the War on Drugs in numbers

www.drugpolicy.org/wasted-tax-dollars

www.countthecosts.org

www.emcdda.europa.eu/countries/compare

www.ons.gov.uk/ons/rel/subnational-health3/deaths-related-to-drug-poisoning/england-and-wales---2014/deaths-related-to-drug-poisoning-in-england-and-wales--2014-registrations.html

www.gro-scotland.gov.uk/news/2015/drug-related-deaths-in-scotland-in-2014

www.talkingdrugs.org/interactive-map-drugs-and-the-death-penalty

www.amnesty.org.uk/world-executions-death-sentences-2014

www.amnesty.org/en/latest/campaigns/2015/10/is-the-death-penalty-the-answer-to-drug-crime/

www.unodc.org/documents/drugs/printmaterials2013/NPS_leaflet/WDC13_NPS_leaflet_EN_LORES.pdf

www.hrw.org/sites/default/files/reports/HHR%20Drug%20Detention%20Brochure_LOWRES.pdf

www.ihra.net/global-state-of-harm-reduction

www.naacp.org/pages/criminal-justice-fact-sheet

www.emcdda.europa.eu/countries/portugal

www.tdpf.org.uk/blog/success-portugal%E2%80%99s-decriminalisation-policy-%E2%80%93-seven-charts

www.globalresearch.ca/cocaine-heroin-cannabis-ecstasy-how-big-is-the-global-drug-trade/5381210

www.unodc.org/unodc/en/drug-trafficking/west-and-central-africa.html

www.drugpolicy.org/resource/just-slap-wrist-life-changing-consequences-marijuana-arrest

www.drugpolicy.org/drug-war-statistics

www.pbs.org/wgbh/frontline/article/the-staggering-death-toll-of-mexicos-drug-war/

www.ihra.net/files/2015/10/07/DeathPenaltyDrugs_Report_2015.pdf

www.cdc.gov/mmwr/preview/mmwrhtml/mm6221a3.htm

www.who.int/injection_safety/about/resources/BackInfoUnsafe/en/

edition.cnn.com/2013/09/02/world/americas/mexico-drug-war-fast-facts/

www.undrugcontrol.info/en/issues/human-rights/item/4144-the-death-penalty-for-drug-offences

https://fas.org/sgp/crs/row/RL34215.pdf

Additional sources from essays

Ernesto Zedillo

Page 24   **some people become addicted to drugs:** See http://www.drugabuse.gov/publications/drugs-brains-behavior-science-addiction/drug-abuse-addiction

Page 24   **most likely unachievable, level:** For proof of this proposition see: Becker, Gary S., Kevin M. Murphy and Michael Grossman, 'The Economic Theory of Illegal Goods: The Case of Drug,' Working Paper 10976 (National Bureau of Economic Research, 2004) http://www.nber.org/papers/w10976.pdf

Page 26   **might attack white society:** Musto, David F. (1996) *The American Disease: Origins of Narcotic Control*. New York: Oxford University Press, p. 6.

Page 26   **discriminatory voting laws:** Musto, *The American Disease*, p. 7.

Page 26   **may commit crime in order to obtain it:** Musto, *The American Disease*, p. 138.

Page 26   **violation of federal narcotic laws:** For example, the Webb case of 1919 was an appeal brought to the Supreme Court by a physician and a pharmacist who had been convicted of supplying drugs to an addict to support his addiction for the reason that addiction is a disease and one that requires indefinite maintenance. Musto, David F., *Drugs in America: A Documentary History*, pp. 256 and 265.

Page 26   **with growing and smoking cannabis:** Musto, *Drugs in America*, p. 189.

Page 26   **crimes of violence and marijuana:** Musto, *Drugs in America*, p. 453.

Page 27   **a menace wherever it is purveyed:** Musto, *Drugs in America*, p. 459.

Page 27   **narcotics and the drug problem:** Musto, *The American Disease*, p. 232.

Page 27   **hardly be called a controversial one**: Musto, *Drugs in America*, p. 285.

Page 27   **committed by addicts:** Musto, *Drugs in America*, p. 285.

Page 27   **'crackpot' doctors and sociologists:** Musto, *The American Disease*, p. 233.

Page 28   **the US federal government:** *Quest for Drug Control*, p. 8

Page 28   **President Nixon addressed the US congress on the issue of illegal drugs:** In the 'Special Message to the Congress on Control of Narcotics and Dangerous Drugs' (14 July 1969) President Nixon did not use the term 'war on drugs' but he clearly, and in great detail, outlined the policy that would be in effect for the duration of his administration. (http://www.presidency.ucsb.edu/ws/index. php?pid=2126). It was in a press conference in June 1971 that he first identified drug abuse as 'public enemy number one' and declared that 'In order to fight and defeat this enemy, it is necessary to wage a new, all-out offensive.'

Page 29   **our standing in the polls on those:** *Quest for Drug Control*, p. 264, footnote 16.

Page 29   **despite what the commission has recommended:** *Quest for Drug Control*, pp. 114–15.

Page 30   **compared with 300,000 in 1972:** See Stevenson, Bryan, 'Drug Policy, Criminal Justice and Mass Imprisonment', (2011) Document prepared for the Global Commission on Drug Policies.

Page 31   **in three United Nations Conventions:** The three are the 'Single Convention on Narcotic Drugs, 1961', United Nations (http://www.unodc.org/pdf/convention_1961_en.pdf), the 'Convention on Psychotropic Substances, 1971', United Nations (http://www.unodc.org/pdf/convention_1971_en.pdf), and 'United Nations Convention Against Illicit Traffic in Narcotic Drugs and Psychotropic Substances, 1988', United Nations (http://www.unodc.org/pdf/convention_1988_en.pdf)

Page 31   **seems to have been rather modest:** Mejía, Daniel (2010), 'The War on Drugs under Plan Colombia', in Zedillo, Ernesto, and Haynie, Wheeler, eds, *Rethinking the 'War on Drugs' Through the US–Mexico Prism* (New Haven: Yale Center for the Study of Globalization, 2012)

Page 32 **between December 2006 and November 2015:** Provided directly to this author by Eduardo Guerrero stating as his main sources: Figures from December 2006 to December 2010 from *Base de Datos de Fallecimientos Ocurridos por Presunta Rivalidad Delincuencial*, Presidencia de la República. From January 2011 to September 2011, from the report *Fallecimientos Ocurridos por Presunta Rivalidad Delincuencial*, Procuraduría General de la República. From October 2011 to November 2015 from various open sources identified by *Lantia Consultores*.

Page 34 **by existing Mexican laws:** For an independent assessment of those drug policies see: Guerrero, Eduardo, 'Políticas de seguridad en México: análisis de cuatro sexenios', chapter in Aguayo, Sergio, and Raul Benitez Manaut, editores, *Atlas de la Seguridad y la Defensa de México 2012*, Colectivo de Análisis de la Seguridad con Democracia A. C. México, 2012.

Page 37 **including the UNODC:** UNODC, Briefing Paper: 'Decriminalization of Drug Use and Possession for Personal Consumption'. This document was brought to my attention by Sir Richard Branson and can be found in his blog webpage (http://www.virgin.com/richard-branson/finally-a-change-in-course-on-drug-policy).

Page 37 **or proffering such policy alternatives:** Transform Drug Policy Foundation, *After the War on Drugs: A Blueprint for Regulation*, UK, 2009.

Ruth Dreifuss

Page 60 **In 2015 Indonesia executed 14 people** http://www.nytimes.com/2015/04/29/world/asia/indonesia-execution.html?emc=edit_th_20150429&nl=todaysheadlines&nlid=40992186&_r=2

Page 60 **Saudi Arabia executed at least 175 people** http://www.theguardian.com/world/2015/aug/25/saudi-arabia-executed-175-people-amnesty-international

Page 60 **At least 13 countries** http://www.undrugcontrol.info/en/issues/human-rights/item/4144-the-death-penalty-for-drug-offences

Page 61 **the death penalty demonstrably fails to deter crime** http://
theconversation.com/there-is-no-evidence-that-the-death-penalty-
acts-as-a-deterrent-37886

Page 62 **The UN Human Rights Council** http://www.ohchr.org/
Documents/HRBodies/HRCouncil/DrugProblem/Reprieve.pdf

Page 62 **routinely denounced for committing human
rights violations** http://www.un.org/apps/news/story.
asp?NewsID=50238#.VnQ0Lkj72jM

Page 63 **From the United Nations General Assembly** https://
www.unodc.org/ungass2016/

Fernando Henrique Cardoso

Page 96 **in Brazil:** Criminalisation of drugs still endures in Venezuela, El
Salvador, Guatemala, Honduras, Belize and in my own country, Brazil.
For more information, see http://www.justica.gov.br/noticias/senad-
divulga-levantamento-sobre-legislacao-de-drogas-nas-americas-e-
europa

Page 96 **some link to the war on drugs**: Freiser, V., and Oliveira, A., '56,
12% dos homicídios no Brasil tem ligação direta com o tráfico',
Primeira Hora Notícias, 13 Sep. 2011. Available at: <http://www.
primeirahoranoticias.com.br/mato_grosso/4989/5612+dos+homicidi
os+no+Brasil+tem+ligacao+direta+com+o+trafico.+Centro+Oste+e
+Campeao+na+Criminalidade>. Accessed on 30th October 2015.

Page 96 **over the last decade:** (UNODC 2012. World Drug Report, Vienna)
https:// www.unodc.org/documents/data-and-analysis/WDR2012/
WDR_2012_web_small.pdf

Page 96 **individual countries' production:** UNODC 2012. World Drug
Report, Vienna) https:// www.unodc.org/documents/data-and-
analysis/WDR2012/ WDR_2012_web_small.pdf

Page 96 **drug production moving elsewhere:** *The Economist* 'Why is
less cocaine coming from Colombia?', 2 April 2013. www.economist.
com/blogs/economist-explains/2013/04/economist-explains-
whycolombia-produces-less-cocaine

Page 98 **once in the previous year:** (UNODC, 2012. World Drug Report,
Vienna) https:// www.unodc.org/documents/data-and-analysis/
WDR2012/ WDR_2012_web_small.pdf

Page 98   **have grown steadily:** UNECOSOC, 2007, *World Situation with Regard to Drug Abuse: Report of the Commission on Narcotic Drugs*, March. www.unodc.org/pdf/cnd_session/ECN72007_3E.pdf

Page 99   **and economic growth:** UNODC (United Nations Office on Drugs and Crime), 2007, *Crime and Development in Central America: Caught in the Crossfire*, Vienna: UNODC. www.unodc.org/documents/data-and-analysis/Central-america-study-en.pdf

Page 100   **basic health services:** *Count the Costs: 50 Years of the War on Drugs. 2012. Undermining Human Rights.* ‹http://www.countthecosts.org/sites/default/files/Human_rights_briefing.pdf›

Page 100   **have been devastating:** Global Commission on Drug Policy, 2011, *Report of the Global Commission on Drug Policy*, June. www. globalcommissionondrugs.org/wp-content/themes/gcdp_v1/pdf/Global_Commission_Report_English.pdf

Page 100   **regions at war:** Waiselfisz, Julio, 2008, *Mapa da violência: os jovens da América Latina*, RITLA, Ministério da Justiça do Brasil and Instituto Sangari. Artecor Gráfica e Editora. ‹http://www. mapadaviolencia. org.br/publicacoes/Mapa_2008_al.pdf›; Waiselfisz, Julio, 2012, *Mapa da violência 2012: os novos padrões da violência homicida no Brasil*, Instituto Sangari. www.sangari.com/mapadaviolencia/pdf2012/mapa2012_web.pdf

Page 100   **in the favelas:** UNECOSOC (United Nations Economic and Social Council). Commission on Human Rights, 2004, *Civil and Political Rights, Including the Question of Disappearances and Summary Executions: Extrajudicial, Summary or Arbitrary Executions: Report of the Special Rapporteur, Asma Jahangir*, www.refworld.org/docid/3b00f5540.html

Page 101   **we used to endorse:** In 2011 the originally Latin American initiative became global and the Global Commission on Drug Policy – GCDP – was born.

Page 103   **the community at large:** UNDP, *Addressing the Development Dimensions of Drug Policy*, June 2015. www.undp.org/content/dam/undp/library/HIV-AIDS/Discussion-Paper--Addressing-the-Development-Dimensions-of-Drug-Policy.pdf

Page 103   **against users more generally:** Human Rights Council, UN Doc. A/HRC/30/65

Page 103 **recommendations of possible outcomes:** UNU, *What Comes After the War on Drugs – Flexibility, Fragmentation or Principles Pluralism.*

Olusegun Obasanjo

Page 123 **essay epigraph:** From 'We Are People – The unintended consequences of the Nigerian Drug Law on the health and human rights of young people who use drugs'. Youth RISE, January 2015.

Page 123 **10 countries in West Africa:** For more information visit www.wacommissionondrugs.org

Professor Carl L. Hart

Page 138 **at similar rates:** Edwards, E., Bunting W., and Garcia, L. (2013) 'The War on Marijuana in Black and White'. American Civil Liberties Union report, June 2013; www.samhsa.gov/data/sites/default/files/NSDUHresultsPDFWHTML2013/Web/NSDUHresults2013.pdf

Page 140 **users of the drug were white:** United States Sentencing Commission. Special Report to the Congress – Cocaine and Federal Sentencing Policy, February 1995.

Page 141 **or an ethical perspective:** Hart, C. L. (2013) *High Price: A neuroscientist's journey of self-discovery that challenges everything you know about drugs and society.* HarperCollins: New York.

Page 141 **federal crack cocaine law:** United States Sentencing Commission. Special Report to the Congress – Impact of the Fair Sentencing Act of 2010, August 2015.

Page 142 **death penalty for drug trafficking:** Gallahue, P., and Lines, R. (2010) 'The Death Penalty for Drug Offences: Global Overview 2010'. International Harm Reduction Association: /www.deathpenaltyinfo.org/new-resources-death-penalty-drug-offences-global-overview-2010

Page 143 **drug law violations are black:** Federal Bureau of Investigation (2014), *Crime in the United States 2013.* Available at: www.fbi.gov/about-us/cjis/ ucr/crime-in-the-u.s/2013/crime-in-the-u.s.-2013/tables/ table-43

Page 143 **of the incarcerated population:** http://www.bjs.gov/content/pub/pdf/p13.pdf

Page 143 **this damning prospect:** Bonzcar, T. P. (2003) 'Prevalence of imprisonment in the U.S. population, 1974–2001'. D.o.J. Bureau of Justice Statistics, Editor 2003: Washington, DC.

Page 144 **including the UK:** Eastwood, N., Shiner M., and Bear, D. (2013), *The numbers in black and white: ethnic disparities in the policing and prosecution of drug offences in England and Wales*. Release Publications. http://www.release.org.uk/sites/default/files/pdf/publications/Release%20-%20Race%20Disparity%20Report%20final%20version.pdf; **and Brazil:** Hart, C. L. (2015) 'Empty slogans, real problems'. *Sur International Journal of Human Rights* 12(21).http://www.release.org.uk/sites/default/files/pdf/publications/Release – Race Disparity Report final version.pdf

Pavel Bém

Page 164 **In combination, these policies:** *European Drug Report 2014: Trends and Developments*. EMCDDA. Luxembourg: Publication Office of the EU; Annual Report Czech Republic – Drug Situation 2012, 2013. Office of the Government. Czech Republic. 2013

Page 165 **Immediately after the parliamentary vote:** ZábranskýT., Mravčík V., Gajdošíková H. and Miovský M. (2001) PAD: Impact Analysis Project of New Drugs Legislation (Summary Final Report). Prague: ResAd/Scan. 80-86620-02-6 (English version).

Page 166 **The Impact Analysis Project:** Zábranský, T., and Rasmussen, D.R., Cost and Benefit Analysis of the Implementation of Penalization of Possession of Illegal Drugs for Personal Use in the Czech Republic in 2000. Adiktologie suppl. 191-207. Prague, 2002.

Peter Dunne

Page 174 **a new regime with its own criteria and approval process for regulating new substances:** *Controlling and Regulating Drugs: a review of the Misuse of Drugs Act 1975*, p142, New Zealand Law Commission, www.lawcom.govt.nz

Acknowledgements

I wish to thank all those who have contributed to this effort. My editors at Virgin Books, Ed Faulkner and Lydia Good and Virgin's Matthias Stausberg, who expertly corralled the contributors and has helped me bring the book to life. Special thanks go to Danny Kushlick, Martin Powell, Steve Rolles, and Nicky Saunter of Transform Drug Policy Foundation for their expert review, while Zara Snapp, Ilona Szabó de Carvalho, and Dr Khalid Tinasti of the Secretariat of the Global Commission on Drug Policy (www.globalcommissionondrugs.org) were instrumental in giving structure to this book. But I'm most grateful to the 12 authors whose writing allows only one conclusion: the War on Drugs must end, and we must review and reform our drug policies so that people around the world are safe, criminal gangs are put out of business and doctors are free to help those who need it.

Sir Richard Branson

Index

This book was made possible with generous support from Virgin Unite

Virgin Unite is the entrepreneurial foundation of the Virgin Group and the Branson family. We started Virgin Unite with the aim of bringing people together to encourage them never to accept the unacceptable, to turn challenges into opportunities and to always push boundaries that make both business and the world better.

Our goal is to unite people and entrepreneurial ideas to create opportunities for a better world. There are so many challenges facing the world today, but we believe that by bringing the right people together and taking an entrepreneurial approach, we can create positive change.

Our work is divided into four areas:

- **Changing business for good** – We believe business can be a driving force for social, environmental and economic benefit.

- **Market solutions to address climate change and conserve our natural resources** – We believe businesses have a big part to play in creating opportunities from the challenges we face.

- **The power of entrepreneurs** – We help early stage entrepreneurs build credible business plans for growth that have a positive impact in the world.

- **Human dignity** – We work to protect every human's basic rights and freedoms through shining a spotlight on issues that we feel are unacceptable.

For more information please visit www.virginunite.com